Answers From Inside

The Must-Read Business Law FAQs for Entrepreneurs

Richard Wayne Bobholz

Law++

<u>**DEDICATION**</u>

This book is dedicated to the small businesses that keep our economy moving. This is for the entrepreneur who leads the charge with a handshake. This is for the inventor who is all too familiar with the late night crunch. This is for the salesperson who redefined what it means to hustle. This is for you.

Without you, the small business owner, this book would not be possible. I could only create this book because of all the great questions you asked in the quest to protect your dream. As an attorney and a business owner, I thrive on my clients' and colleagues' energy, courage, and drive. You've given me these beyond what I could imagine.

Thank you.

TABLE OF CONTENTS

INTRODUCTION

How to Use This Book

This book is your handy guide to a better understanding of the practice of law as well as getting those most commonly asked questions taken care of without a large invoice coming to you. It is merely an educational tool and not legal advice. Nor is this book meant to create any sort of attorney-client relationship. I cannot provide any advice or agree to take on a client without knowing about your situation.

Certain sections of this book are very useful for holding your attorney accountable, but most of the book is for general business law knowledge.

The book is separated out into logical sections, each of which is listed in the table of contents. From there, I arranged the questions in logical groupings in the order they are most received.

There is also an index in case there are specific terms you are looking for. Definitions in this book are my definitions for the circumstances that come up in my practice; therefore, they may not apply to what you're looking for. For example, an officer means something different in a nonprofit, a for profit, and outside of a business scenario. There are many other resources for defining terms such as Black's Law Dictionary or Dictionary.com. In many circumstances the colloquial meaning and the legal meaning are very different, so just be cautious when comparing sources.

This is the first edition of this book, and as you continue to ask me more questions, I will provide updated versions for you. The goal is to create an ongoing and affordable resource for you to get answers to these commonly asked questions.

All of the questions in this book are catered towards North Carolina law though I wrote the answers in a way to attempt to make them more broadly applicable, when possible.

If you are another professional and have clients that ask these questions, please feel free to use these answers and cite my book. If your clients have follow up questions, please consider referring them to me for those answers. If you receive a lot of the same questions over the course of your professional career, please send those questions my way, and I will try to include as many answers as I can in later editions of this book.

About Richard Bobholz

Richard Bobholz is the Managing Attorney at Law++ in Durham, North Carolina. Richard is an author, an attorney, a speaker, and an avid community volunteer.

Richard wanted to become a lawyer because he wanted to help others. The thought of being there for people has always been an appeal of his, and when it comes to the law, his mindset and his desire to learn make him an exceptional attorney. Outside the legal realm, Richard enjoys running, programming websites and applications, exploring the Triangle Area in North Carolina, and spending time with his friends and family.

Throughout his life, Richard has scarcely been without a new topic to learn. Whether it is details about a client's business or a useful skill, Richard tries to keep his mind finely tuned at all times.

When it comes to loyalty and dedication, Law++ is second to none. Any attorney can file articles with the Secretary of State, but Richard keeps you on his mind. If you start a business, Richard can file the proper papers for you and then continue to think of ways to improve your business. He also knows the value of making introductions to those who can bring value to your company. When you choose to work with Law++, you buy more than just legal services. You gain a relationship with a trusted, skilled, adviser.

Because those who are exceptional should use their skills to help others, Richard continues to find ways to help low-income individuals, nonprofit corporations, and those with disabilities pro bono as often as possible.

About Law++

Law++ is a revolutionary and award-winning law firm based in Durham, NC. The firm represents businesses, individuals, and professionals throughout the Triangle area.

Ranging from contracts to mergers and acquisitions, the firm operates as general counsel for small businesses. In an effort to ensure that smaller issues are taken care of promptly, clients are able to take advantage of a monthly subscription program that is affordable enough to encourage regular contact with Law++ attorneys.

Law++ is primarily a small business law firm, but it also offers limited estate planning and asset protection services for business owners and individuals who need these.

One of the firm's claims to fame is the almost exclusive use of flat rate billing. Richard Bobholz runs the statistics on every service offered to ensure that he can provide an upfront cost for the most common services a business or individual may need the firm to do. The most common services with their prices are listed online.

How You Can Help

I made this guide to help as many people as possible. In order to reach a wider audience, I need your assistance to reach those who would benefit from this guide.

If you know someone who has questions about working with a business attorney or someone who is thinking about hiring a business attorney, please recommend this book. When you are finished with your copy, please feel free to pass this book to your friends and colleagues as well!

I sincerely appreciate you for reading this and anyone who bought a copy. I put a lot of time and effort into making this book, though the effect it could have for you kept me motivated.

Got other Questions?

I became an attorney because I love the law. I love knowing and practicing the law. Therefore, if you have questions this book has not addressed, please feel free to ask me at richard@lawplusplus.com. Due to the nature of my business, it may take me a couple of days to respond. If the question is one that should be in this book, I may answer it for free. If not, I will let you know, and if you're interested, we can schedule a phone conversation or meeting to go over your situation.

I sincerely appreciate all your feedback!

ROLE OF AN ATTORNEY

What does an attorney do for a small business?

Hiring an attorney can be useful in a wide variety of areas, but ultimately, what an attorney can do for your small business depends on your needs and your wants. The only limitations are that the tasks must be legal and not in violation of the Rules of Professional Conduct of any state where that attorney is licensed. If your attorney is willing to do it, and you're willing to pay, you can have your attorney pick up your dry cleaning.

Some more specific things attorneys are typically hired for include setting up the LLC or corporation, drafting or reviewing contracts, setting up or enforcing employment policies, protecting your company's intellectual property, suing on your behalf, defending lawsuits on your behalf, or conducting the process of buying, selling, or merging companies.

Attorneys are also great sounding boards for ideas or concerns you have. They're qualified to listen for the important details, spot the problems, and help solve the problems with their training and experience. Additionally, there is a built in confidentiality with the attorney-client relationship.

What does "conflict of interest" mean?

A conflict of interest is a concept that exists in everyday life, but is something very specific when dealing with attorney's Rules of Professional Conduct. In North Carolina, conflicts of interest are covered by Rules 1.7 & 1.8. Broadly speaking, an attorney may not represent a client if that representation would force the attorney to represent both sides to a dispute or negotiation. The rules get into far more specifics, including exceptions to the rule and more guidance on specific circumstances.

The most important thing to know is that if your attorney obtains information from you, he or she may not use that information against you on behalf of another client, even in the future, unless you give your permission.

It is, however, not a conflict of interest for an attorney to use information you gave him or her to file a lawsuit against you for a dispute you would have with your lawyer.

What's with those disclaimers on attorney websites?

You're probably referring to a couple of specific disclaimers that you see repeatedly on attorney and law firm websites.

The first one essentially states that any information posted on the website is for educational purposes only and does not, or was not intended to, constitute legal advice. This is a required disclaimer anytime a lawyer has a blog or any piece of content that could be used by a potential client. Basically, this covers anything useful on a lawyer's website.

Lawyers have to ensure that they protect themselves from the "accidental client." The accidental client is a person who thought they were receiving legal advice from the lawyer and that they were represented by this lawyer. That's also why, a lot of the time, you'll ask a lawyer a question in public and his or her answers will be utterly useless for you.

This disclaimer means that anything you do with the information you've gained is your problem, and you cannot turn around and sue the attorney because you used the information without any legal guidance. Lawyers may only be sued for malpractice by clients or heirs and assigns of clients. Therefore, no client means no lawsuit. This is the case even if you suffered harm because you relied on information provided by that lawyer's blog.

The other major disclaimer is the one that states that there is no attorney-client relationship, nor any duty of confidentiality, until an engagement letter has been signed by both the attorney and the client. This one is important for you to understand because there may be implications to you.

One of the most important reasons an attorney puts this disclaimer on his or her website is when he or she has a contact form on the site. Without the disclaimer, the attorney runs the risk of being conflicted out of other cases merely because you sent a long message in that contact form outlining all of the facts (good or bad) of your case.

Both of these disclaimers seek to ensure that you realize that you are not a client until that attorney says you are a client. This generally includes agreeing to some fee because most attorneys do not work for free.

What are attorney rules of ethics?

These are also called Rules of Professional Conduct. These are the rules established by the North Carolina State Bar and the Supreme Court of North Carolina that every attorney who is licensed in North Carolina must follow. Any violation of these rules may be reported to the State Bar by any person.

The punishments for violations of these rules vary depending on the violation and surrounding circumstances. The one thing that will always get an attorney disbarred is embezzling from the lawyer's trust account (IOLTA Account). The other punishments range from an informal, non-public, reprimand to fines, suspension, and disbarment.

Since the rules do not cover absolutely every scenario, there are also published ethics opinions. These ethics opinions take a specific set of facts and provide a precedential ruling on what should happen under those facts. The ethics opinions are equally as enforceable against attorneys as the rules themselves. They, however, operate much like Appellate or Supreme Court cases in that they can be expanded upon or overruled by later ethics opinions, or updates to the rules themselves.

Ultimately, these rules are law for attorneys just like the criminal statutes are law for everyone. If you want to know more about them, all the rules and ethics opinions are listed on the North Carolina State Bar's website. Other states publish their rules as well.

You can also use the State Bar website to search for attorneys and their disciplinary records. In the attorney directory, every non-private punishment will be listed in that attorney's profile.

How do attorneys bill?

The most common way for a private attorney to bill is hourly. Attorneys bill from a hundred to thousands of dollars per hour, depending on the practice area, skill, demand, and other facts regarding the attorney.

Another way attorneys bill is on commission or contingency. This is more common in personal injury cases like slip & falls or insurance claims than other practice areas. In exchange for representation on the case, the client agrees to give the attorney a percentage of the total outcome. If the attorney loses the case, the client generally owes nothing. There are variations of this commission where the client owes a certain amount of fees or costs throughout the process as well. The fee agreement will outline any costs.

Attorneys can also bill as a flat rate, subscription ("retainer"), or some hybrid of any of the above types of billing. A flat rate means you pay one price for a set product or service. Subscription is a monthly price for ongoing services.

Attorneys can require an advance payment as well. In legal terms, this is frequently called a retainer payment, but that term can mean a variety of things.

"Retainer" can be used to mean a nonrefundable fee simply to begin representation, a monthly fee for service, or an advance payment. Be sure to clarify if your attorney mentions a retainer.

Attorneys may also require interest or fees for late payments, reasonable attorney fees for collection efforts, and other payment terms to ensure timely payments, just like any other business.

What can I do if I think my attorney did a bad job?

Attorneys are professionals who rely on their education, experience, and their effort to do a quality job. Therefore, unfortunately, they can make mistakes. There are two types of mistakes that can be made: ethical and professional.

When there is an ethical mistake, you can bring an ethics complaint against the attorney through the State Bar. This is a free process, but it rarely gets the client any money back or any sort of better result. This process is similar to reporting someone for breaking a law.

When an attorney makes a professional mistake, this is called malpractice. Different states have different standards for how to prove malpractice. In North Carolina, in order to prove malpractice, you essentially have to show that you would have had a better outcome without the mistake made by the attorney. Certain mistakes are almost always malpractice, like missed appellate deadlines or statute of limitations that prevent your case from moving forward.

For malpractice, you need to file a lawsuit against the attorney for malpractice. Generally, this involves hiring a new attorney. Most every attorney has malpractice insurance to protect him or herself from these types of mistakes. This insurance also protects the client.

What can I do if I believe my attorney has overbilled me?

Attorneys are not permitted to charge for work they did not do, nor charge you "excessive fees." If you believe your attorney charged for work that was not done, this is a clearer violation than just excessive fees. The difference lies in proving the work wasn't done versus proving the attorney was not worth the amount billed.

In order to address either of these complaints, you can use the State Bar's fee dispute resolution program. https://www.ncbar.gov/public/alternatives.asp

The fee dispute resolution program is free for clients to use, and participation is mandatory for attorneys. The program is more of a mediation program than an actual enforceable judgment against your attorney. The program may result in ethics violations against the attorney if the charges are severe enough.

You may also file a lawsuit for breach of contract against an attorney you believe overbilled you. You may do this before or after using the fee dispute resolution program, but the lawsuit will cost you money.

Note: Some of these fee dispute cases have shown that even $1,000 per hour is not excessive in the right circumstances.

Can I fire my attorney?

Yes. You may fire your attorney at any time for any reason. Your attorney may however be entitled to some fees upon termination of the attorney-client relationship regardless of the billing situation.

Why are attorney answers always so unhelpful?

Lawyers answers are supposed to be calculated, educational, and meant to give you all the information necessary to allow you to make a decision.

Because attorneys rarely should be making decisions for you, their advice frequently comes off as unhelpful, especially when it is a tougher decision that you need to make.

If the advice is ever incomplete or does not make sense, you should certainly ask your attorney for more information. If, however, you're looking for your attorney to make a decision for you, you will frequently be disappointed.

Most times, an attorney's answer feels unhelpful because it is designed to avoid certainty. Much like how this book is written, there are very few absolutes in the law. Therefore, attorneys can't easily provide definitive answers. The more information the attorney has, the more specific the answers can be; however, attorneys unfortunately cannot predict what other people or the courts will do.

What is pro bono?

Pro bono is free legal work provided by an attorney, generally to good causes or persons with limited means. Attorneys can provide pro bono on their own or through organizations such as Legal Aid.

Attorneys, at least in NC, are never required to provide pro bono work, and they're also allowed to attach strings to their offerings of pro bono services.

How can I get an attorney to help me pro bono?

Attorneys are not required to provide pro bono work to you, so getting an attorney to provide you with free help isn't always easy.

If you're suffering some greater legal harm and have a lower income or hard economic situation, you can contact organizations such as Legal Aid to find a volunteer attorney to help you. Getting pro bono help for businesses is much more difficult. There are organizations such as NC LEAP that provide pro bono attorneys for entrepreneurs with low income and low wealth, but these business oriented organizations do not exist in every state.

Many educational resources suggest that nonprofits can regularly get attorneys to help pro bono. Many can, but obtaining a qualified business or nonprofit attorney to help a nonprofit pro bono is more difficult than obtaining an attorney in certain other practice areas where there are programs like legal aid to help.

Also keep in mind that many of the attorneys who are offering pro bono services are not as qualified in those areas as others. Be sure you're still getting quality work from an attorney familiar with that practice area. Sometimes you can do the work just as well as an unfamiliar attorney.

What things should I ask before hiring an attorney?

Hiring an attorney is a very important decision that should not be taken lightly. Before committing to a particular attorney, be sure to get all the answers you need to make the best decision possible.

First and foremost, ensure that you can trust your attorney. Ask about his or her experience in situations like yours.

Ask about your attorney's policies, practices, and billing to ensure you understand contractually what it will be like working with this attorney. You should also ask about your attorney's values to be sure that you know what working with your attorney will be like.

Before hiring your attorney, be sure to read the contract you will be signing with him or her. Ask questions about it, and if necessary, take it home with you to think it over.

Some more specific questions should include the following:
1) When can I expect my work to be completed?
2) Who can I contact if I can't reach you?
3) Am I billed for phone calls or follow up questions about work prepared for me?
4) Are you strictly a business lawyer or do you practice in more areas?
5) How often should I expect updates?
6) What should I expect to pay for this service?
7) How can I keep my bill lower?
8) Will I be working with you or another attorney or paralegal mostly?
9) Who will be doing the work on my case?

These questions are very important, and if your lawyer cannot answer any of them to your satisfaction, that should be a major red flag. Just like any relationship, this should fit what you're looking for. If you have to settle for less than you expected, you'll be dissatisfied with the relationship.

Do attorneys charge a consultation fee?

Sometimes. Lawyers are permitted to charge a consultation fee if they want. You should find out before the consultation if your lawyer is going to be charging this fee. If the attorney does charge a consultation fee, everything you discuss during the meeting will be protected under attorney-client privilege. If you are not charged a consultation fee, you will still have a confidentiality protection, but to a lesser extent.

What can I do to make sure my attorney is meeting deadlines?

Lawyers are notoriously busy and have a reputation for being difficult to get to respond. If/when this happens to you, there are ways to be proactive to ensure you're a top priority without being too interruptive of your attorney's work.

First and foremost, ask up front when your lawyer believes your work will be done or when to expect milestones or deliverables. There's nothing wrong with asking this and holding your attorney to these goals.

Second, feel free to ask if you can get regular updates. Depending on your case or situation, these can be weekly, monthly, or every couple of months. Most aspects of the law do not move quickly, so the need for more frequent updates than this would be unnecessary.

Finally, hold your attorney to the deadlines that are set. If they need to be changed for legitimate reasons, allow the change, but otherwise, these deadlines should be hard and fast. Your attorney should respect your deadlines if he or she respects you as a client.

How are lawyers qualified?

There are several ways in which a lawyer is considered qualified. First, every lawyer in nearly every state has had to attend an American Bar Association accredited law school. These schools follow a set of rules to ensure that their graduates took a certain curriculum and met attendance and minimum performance requirements.

After graduating law school, all attorneys must pass the bar exam in the state they want to practice. Patent attorneys must pass the patent bar, a completely separate bar exam. Attorneys who have not passed the patent bar may not advise their clients on patent matters, nor may they file anything patent related with the US Patent and Trademark Office.

After passing the bar exam in the state the attorney practices, attorneys are required to take continuing legal education courses (CLEs) every year. Some states require attorneys to receive a certain number of these courses in ethics, technology, or substance abuse topics. The rest can be on any area the attorney wishes to learn. There is also nothing preventing the attorney from taking the same CLE multiple years in a row.

More important than the CLEs is the attorney's learned experience. In order to practice in a particular area, an attorney is ethically required to maintain a level of competency to not prejudice their clients. This theoretically means that attorneys study and become comfortable with a practice area before starting to represent clients in that area.

Personally, I shadowed mentoring attorneys, filed my own corporations, spent days observing in court, read nearly every ethics opinion, and hundreds of court cases in order to gain the initial competency in my practice areas. Beyond that, I only take on tasks that are within my base of knowledge and am constantly learning to become better. This does not mean attorneys should have every answer readily available to him or her. Rather, it means your attorney should know the issues and how to find the answers.

I used the word "learned" earlier because a lot of attorneys (and other professionals) do not constantly learn. Experience means nothing when the experience is not learned from. In order to ensure your attorney is qualified, you must be sure that he or she has a significant amount of learned experience. An attorney who learned for a year will likely be better for you than an attorney who has learned nothing for 40 years. That's an extreme example, but something to think about.

Another important consideration for the experience portion of an attorney's qualification is to ensure that he or she has experience in the area you need them to be experienced in. Because of the vast amount of knowledge an attorney needs to know in their specific practice area, it makes it hard for a generalist to be knowledgeable in the specific area you need them to be. For example, you shouldn't hire your real estate attorney to conduct your business acquisition. For the same reasons, you should not hire Law++ to conduct your real estate closing, family law matter, bankruptcy, or anything outside of our practice areas.

What are lawyer specialties and what does that mean?

Lawyer specialties are somewhat arbitrary distinctions, but they can help you identify someone in the particular area you're looking for. An attorney who specializes in a field is an attorney who has a state bar recognized specialization. In North Carolina, and many other states, this means that the attorney practices primarily in that practice area for a period of years. The attorney must also take a certain number of CLEs in that practice area each year.

I call it a somewhat arbitrary distinction because not everything has a specialty and the requirements are not based on merit, but rather time and technical requirements. I know many attorneys who are not specialists in any area, yet they are some of the best attorneys I know in their respective fields.

The specialist title will help you ensure you're getting an attorney that focuses on that field opposed to being a generalist.

Why can't lawyers say they're experts or specialists?

An attorney, at least in North Carolina, cannot say that he or she is a specialist unless that attorney is a board certified specialists. This protects the public from attorneys misleading them about the specialty status.

Attorneys cannot use the word expert unless they can prove they're an expert in the field they're claiming. This usually requires third party certifications like universities, academic journals, or similarly prestigious sources. The reason is the same as with "specialist." The state bar uses these rules to protect the public from misleading advertising.

Why should I hire a business lawyer versus some other type of lawyer?

Lawyers need to know a lot of information in order to serve you at a competent level. In order to serve you at the exceptional level you deserve, they need to know even more. The vastness is comparable to knowing everything in the engineering profession. The same reason you wouldn't hire a chemical engineer to build a bridge is why you shouldn't hire a criminal attorney to set up your company.

A business lawyer spent a significant amount of time learning business law before taking on his or her first business client. He or she then expanded his or her knowledge through learned experience.

What happens if my attorney dies or disappears in the middle of my case?

Every attorney is required to have a contingency plan for if/when the worst happens. Most don't. Good, regular, communication will hopefully help avoid any problems that may occur if an attorney dies or disappears. You'll at least know if something is wrong when you've missed your regular communication.

If, however, you do suffer harm because your attorney died or disappeared, you may be able to make a claim against your attorney's malpractice insurance, estate, or through the state bar's program specifically set up to protect clients in these circumstances.

What are attorneys not allowed to say in advertisements?

First and foremost, attorneys must be honest and may not deceive in their advertisements. They also may not make any statements that would lead to an expectation of a particular result. For example, an attorney who says "we settle every personal injury case for $1,000,000 or more" would be in violation of this rule. The attorney may not make any statements of fact unless the attorney can prove them.

When making written advertisings, the attorney or law firm must include the phrase "THIS IS AN ADVERTISEMENT FOR LEGAL SERVICES" in the largest font on the page in all capital letters as well as on the outside of the envelop. The attorney or firm must also include the name and address of at least one attorney responsible for the content of the advertisement.

The lawyer or firm may not claim to be specialized or experts in any field unless certified as a specialist by the state bar or an expert by a qualified entity.

Finally, no attorney may directly solicit business over the phone, in person, or by any other means where the attorney and potential client may communicate simultaneously with each other.

Why can't attorneys solicit business?

According to Rule 7.3 of the North Carolina Rules of Professional Conduct, "a lawyer shall not by in-person, live telephone, or real-time electronic contact solicit professional employment when a significant motive for the lawyer's doing so is the lawyer's pecuniary gain, unless the person contact: (1) is a lawyer; or (2) has a family, close personal, or prior professional relationship with the lawyer." This rule protects the public from an onslaught of cold calls and in person requests. It also protects the profession from competition and public image issues.

All written or targeted communications also must follow a specific set of rules in order to ensure they do not mislead or harm the public through their communications.

How does malpractice work?

Malpractice is the cause of action you can claim against your attorney if you believe your attorney did a poor job that negatively affected the outcome of your case or situation. If you think that your attorney committed malpractice in your representation, you should seek out a malpractice attorney to help you understand this cause of action better.

In North Carolina, one of the key elements of attorney malpractice is proving you would have been better off without the attorney's actions you believe amounted to malpractice. This makes malpractice a complicated cause of action.

Can I waive my right to sue my attorney?

In most circumstances, no. If you settle a dispute between you and your attorney, that will be the one main instance where you can waive your right to sue your attorney for causes of action that fell within that dispute.

If an attorney has you waive your right to sue him or her in your fee agreement, this would be unenforceable in almost every circumstance. On top of that, this provision is a red flag.

Along those same lines, attorneys cannot limit their liability or what causes of action you can bring against them. A limitation of liability is essentially a waiver of a portion or all of a claim against that attorney, so it is restricted in the same way as waivers.

__FORMATIONS__

Why do I want to setup a company?

Whether or not you file anything formal with the government, as soon as you start operating for the purpose of making a profit, you have a company. There are likely advantages to operating your business as an LLC or a corporation.

There are three main reasons why you would want to form an LLC or corporation: taxation, liability, or structural benefits. Not all companies receive all three of these, and there are some companies that receive none of these benefits.

There are specific tax codes that people can take advantage of when forming an LLC or corporation. You should talk to a tax professional if you think you may be in one of these categories. Most companies can see at least small savings on business expenses that are otherwise not deductible by a company that isn't an LLC or corporation.

LLCs and corporations provide limited liability protection. What this means is that the actions of the company cannot result in liability to the owners of the company. This, however, does not shield you from actions you take on behalf of the company. For example, if you are a landscaper and damage a client's house, your limited liability protection alone will not protect you because you're the one who caused the harm.

The liability protection does protect against contractual, employee, most premises (slip and fall), and many other types of liability that can come up in the running of your business.

For professionals, where a bulk of the liability comes from the actual work done by the individual, you will have less liability protection reasons to form an LLC or corporation than you have taxation reasons.

The structural benefits frequently result from having to take better care in the course of your business. Just by having an LLC or corporation, you may find that you separate out your business and personal life better. The company structure sometimes also forces a person to think further ahead and keep better records than without the LLC or corporation.

If I'm a sole proprietor, can I start a company?

Yes. In fact, whether you intended to or not, as soon as you start attempting to make a profit, you likely have a company. The alternative is a hobby. The IRS may classify your endeavor as a hobby if you aren't very profitable and otherwise aren't following a significant amount of business formalities.

I heard that setting up a single-member LLC is bad?

Some states have had court cases that ruled that a single-member LLC can be pierced by creditors. These cases were very specific in their rulings, and they do not apply to anyone who is forming a legitimate company. These single-member LLCs were set up solely for asset protection purposes and did not conduct themselves as an ongoing legitimate business.

Other than those limited cases, there have been no issues with forming a single-member LLC. You may want other members for taxation purposes. However, anytime you add another member to your LLC, you give up significant rights

In fact, the only appellate level case in North Carolina where an LLC was breached involved several LLCs that had many members in each one.

What should I consider when starting a company?

That's a loaded question. Answer: Everything. When starting your company, you really need to address how it will run, how you plan on exiting the company, where money will come from, how money will be spent, how you will be paid, and much more.

If you want an incredibly detailed guide on what to consider when starting your company, you should read Check Mark Startup. That book will take you step-by-step on building a company with a great legal and business foundation upon which to build. It doesn't cover every detail, but gets you well on your way.

What is the difference between an LLC and a Corporation?

Especially for small businesses, LLCs and Corporations are more similar than they are different. Both provide limited liability protection. Both require that you file articles with the state you're in. Both have a management structure.

They are, however, unique from a functional and a tax prospective.

Functional

Corporations are distinct legal entities whereas limited liability companies are a collection of their members. Functionally, this makes a huge difference. In the eyes of the law, no one except you cares if you are the owner of a corporation, as they're expected to have many owners who do not necessarily have to participate in the operations of the company. Members of an LLC, however, are managers of the LLC by default. Only through separate contracts do members give up their management authority.

Because of the distinct nature, there are also significant differences between how they operate. Shareholders cannot make management decisions, but they can appoint management. Corporations must also have annual meetings and clear separation of managerial duties.

Taxation

Corporations are taxed as separate legal entities. They stand alone and pay their own taxes. This is sometimes called "double taxation." The corporation pays expenses like any other company. Once those expenses are paid, the corporation pays taxes on whatever profit is left over. If the corporation then pays dividends to owners, those owners pay the dividend tax on those dividends. Unfortunately, dividends are not tax deductible.

In an LLC, owners are taxed on the profits of the company, regardless of whether or not those owners receive the profits. You can contract around how the profits and losses are divided among the members.

Because of the functional differences between the two entity types, when an owner is employed by a corporation, they are considered a W-2 employee. When an owner is employed by an LLC, that owner is considered self-employed for tax and department of labor purposes.

When looking at the tax and functional differences, usually one entity type usually makes more sense than the other. Additionally, there are some very specific reasons why you might choose one or the other that cannot be fully described here. One of the most common of these is for investment properties. LLCs have a phenomenal tax benefit for buying and selling investment properties when done correctly.

Delaware LLCs and Corporations: When should I use them and when shouldn't I?

When they make sense, Delaware LLCs and corporations are remarkable choices for you; however, when they do not make sense, they can really hurt your company to use them.

So, when do they make sense?

If you're running a national or multinational company, there's a good chance you're going to want a Delaware LLC or corporation. Additionally, if you're obtaining a national investor, they may want you to have a company based in Delaware.

Why?

Because Delaware has a great system of laws and courts for business situations. This makes for incredibly predictable results when there are disputes.

Why not?

You likely wouldn't want an out-of-state company when you do business specifically in one state and you're not looking for national investors. When you setup your company in another state, you subject yourself to those laws and that state's jurisdiction. This means, you may have to hire an attorney and travel to that state in case of a lawsuit.

You'd also be required to have an in-state registered agent. These can cost you $25-$200 per month, adding an unnecessary expense to your company. No matter what, you must also file with the state you make the majority of your management decisions in. In the event you form a Delaware company and operate in North Carolina, you will have two separate filings.

Furthermore, professionals rarely want a Delaware or out-of-state LLC or corporation because the professional usually has to get their company approved by their local licensing board.

Where can I find resources for forming an LLC or Corporation?

Shameless plug for Starting Your North Carolina LLC and Starting Your North Carolina Corporation that I published. They can both be found on Amazon, or by scanning the QR codes here.

Beyond those, there are a ton of resources available for people looking to start a company. The SBA has a lot of generic resources, but you'd likely want more state specific ones.

In North Carolina, the Secretary of State's office has a pair of very thorough guides to starting your LLC or corporation. These guides, however, can only give you process information and summations of the rules. They cannot provide legal advice.

The difference between process information and legal advice means, among other things, that the Secretary of State office can tell you what words are reserved words, but they cannot tell you whether or not your choice of name would subject you to risk of trademark infringement.

There are many law firm and business websites that can provide you advice on forming a company. Be warned, however, that this information must be state specific, time specific, and varies based on an individual's set of facts. Government sites are the best for accurate and up-to-date information.

The advantage of a good business attorney is that you know you will be getting the right advice. You also have that attorney's malpractice insurance and state bar ethical rules to protect you. You have no protections from websites or blogs. Online resources also cannot apply your set of facts to a situation.

What is an S corporation?

This is a good question to ask. Countless numbers of soon-to-be-new business owners read somewhere that they should set up an S corporation. When they read this, it means very little because an S corporation is actually only a tax election. It is not separate legal entity.

To be an S corporation you previously filed as an LLC or corporation and then filed Form 2553 to elect to be taxed as an S corporation. To qualify as an S corporation, the legal entity must have fewer than 100 owners, no owners may be companies, all owners must be citizens of the United States, and all equity-based income must be divided based on ownership percentage.

The primary advantage of having the S corporation election is that you get a hybrid partnership and corporation tax treatment. In easier-to-understand terms, this means that after you take a "reasonable salary" as owner and worker in your business, you can pay out equity. The reasonable salary portion is taxed as ordinary income where you pay income tax and FICA. The equity portion is only taxed as equity income, eliminating the FICA tax, and lowering your taxes overall.

What is a tax ID for a company?

Companies have tax IDs just like individuals have tax IDs. In businesses, these are called Employer Identification Numbers (EIN), and they're unique to each business.

How do I get a tax ID for my company?

Obtaining an EIN is actually a very easy process. This is something you do not need to pay someone to do. The whole process takes about 5-10 minutes and you will get your EIN at the end.

To begin the EIN process, you should gather together your approved articles of incorporation or organization and your address, phone number, and personal identification information.

Once you get these things together, you apply online at https://www.irs.gov/businesses/small-businesses-self-employed/apply-for-an-employer-identification-number-ein-online (You can Google Search "IRS EIN" and click the link that is on the IRS.gov website)

Strangely, this process is only available from 7am-10pm Eastern Time. Bizarre!

Errors to look out for:
- If a company previously had the same name as you in the state you're in, you'll likely get an error.

- If you get an error, it is worth trying the process once more in case it was a software error.
- If you get persistent errors, you will have to call the IRS to walk through the longer process.
- You cannot use punctuation except for a couple of characters. Commas and periods are not allowed anywhere on the form.

Can a non-citizen start or own a company in the United States?

Yes, though there will likely be restrictions on working in the business. If you are not a citizen of the United States and you're starting a company, be sure to mention this to your business attorney or immigration attorney.

There may be restrictions on what types of business you may own as well as what role you may play in the business. There may also be restrictions based on sanctions, political issues, or terms of a person's visa.

What other things will I need when setting up an LLC?

To setup an LLC in North Carolina, you need several things:
1. Articles of organization
2. Employer identification number (EIN)
3. Any licenses required for your location and industry
4. Operating agreement
5. Bank account

What other things will I need when setting up a corporation?

To form a corporation in North Carolina, you need several things:
1. Articles of incorporation
2. Employer identification number (EIN)
3. Any licenses required for your location and industry
4. Bylaws
5. Some documentation that grants ownership to you and any other owners

6.   Bank account

What things do I not need when setting up my company?

1.   Stamp or seal
2.   Share ledger
3.   Certificate of existence
4.   Labor law posters (unless you have employees)
5.   Fancy checks (unless you want them)
6.   Registration on any websites or lists

What does "double taxation" mean?

Double taxation is the concept of having to pay federal taxes (sometimes also state taxes) twice on a certain amount of income. This applies when a corporation pays out dividends, but never on salary or other ordinary business expenses.

Because dividends are not allowed to be deducted as a business expense under federal tax law, the corporation pays taxes on the profit that corporation earns and then the owners pay tax on any dividends they receive. In most small businesses, this should never occur because all revenue can be paid out as income or as other expenses.

Can I have multiple types of ownership in my company?

In most cases, yes. In LLCs, you can create as many types of ownership as you'd like simply by describing those ownership types in the operating agreement. In a corporation, you have to create multiple types of stock in your articles, each with its own rights and responsibilities.

You cannot have multiple types of ownership if you elect to be taxed as an S corporation. Some restrictions are fine; however, distributions must be based on equity.

You should be careful when creating different types of ownership. Many times, this is a level of complication that adds significant ambiguity. Ambiguity in legal situations only increases cost.

Furthermore, most states have protective statutes for minority owners or guaranteed rights for all owners in a company.

What are the advantages and disadvantages of a sole proprietorship?

The major advantage to operating as a sole proprietorship is simplicity. There are minimal government filings and all your taxes are reported directly on your 1040. You will still need to obtain licenses and comply with any employment laws.

The major disadvantages to sole proprietorships are liability and taxation. There is usually a better tax treatment in an LLC or corporation for your specific situation. For liability, as a sole proprietor, you are 100% personally liable for any debts of the company, and you can owe these debts for decades. This means that mistakes in your business can cost you your home, your retirement, your car, or other personally owned assets. LLCs and corporations shield you from most of this personal liability.

What is a partnership?

A partnership, sometimes also called a general partnership, is an entity type that is formed when two or more people enter into an arrangement to obtain a profit.

To form a partnership, there are no formal requirements. As soon as two or more people agree to do something to obtain a profit, that entity is automatically formed. A partnership has no limit on how many partners can be in it. The only requirement is that there is more than one. Partners can also be businesses.

The major advantage to a general partnership is the ease in which you can create one. This can also sometimes be a major disadvantage since people end up in accidental partnerships all the time.

The major disadvantage to partnerships is the liability. Like a sole proprietorship, each partner can be held 100% liable for the debts of the company. This means that the actions by one partner can cost the other partners their personal assets like their retirement, home, car, etc.

Should I include my spouse in the ownership of my company?

The answer to this question is an unhelpful "if you want to, yes." There may be tax benefits, but there are no liability or operational benefits to doing so.

Don't listen to anyone who tells you that you're required to have two or more people in an LLC or corporation. They're misinformed. That is one of those legal myths that refuses to die out.

If I have insurance, do I need either an LLC or corporation?

Although there is some overlap between insurance and liability protection from LLCs and corporations, you should still have an LLC or corporation for a couple of reasons.

The first reason for the LLC or corporation is the potential tax benefit. This is something insurance obviously cannot give you.

The second reason is that you get different protection from the limited liability of LLCs or corporations. Insurance has limits and these entities help protect you if these limits are exceeded. LLCs and corporations provide unlimited protection for business debts except in cases of (1) fraudulent transfers or (2) piercing the corporate veil.

If I have an LLC or a corporation, should I get insurance?

Yes. These two fields are complimentary, and depending on your industry, there may be specific insurances that protect you. For example, if you're a professional, you will need malpractice or errors & omissions insurance to protect you from professional negligence. An LLC or corporation does not protect you from malpractice.

Furthermore, the protections from LLCs and corporations come from the extremes. You want insurance to protect you from all the small to mid-sized issues. You're not going to shut down your company over a $25,000 lawsuit, but you also may not have the means to cover that without insurance.

On the flipside, your insurance likely won't cover a $50 million wrongful death claim against you for a slip & fall in your office. In that case, you need the LLC or corporation to shield your personal assets from that claim.

Can I use any of those online companies to form my LLC or corporation?

Can? Yes, but they provide no more usefulness than the Secretary of State's website. If you want to DIY your formation, don't pay some DIY site to help. Instead, just go to the corporation filings division and download their standard form.

If you want or need advice on which type of entity is best for you, or how to complete the form, you'll need to hire professionals to help. The online companies cannot legally offer this type of advice.

Can my bookkeeper, CPA, financial advisor, or other professional setup my company?

You can always ask your professional advisors for advice in their fields; however, under North Carolina law, only attorneys are permitted to file articles of organization or incorporation on behalf of others. Your other professionals cannot help draft or file these on your behalf.

Do I need a certificate of existence?

Probably not. 99% of companies I encounter do not need this. A certificate of existence is useful when filing for a foreign corporation or LLC in another state where they need certification of good standing from your home state. There are other uses, but they are few and far between. To operate a company in North Carolina, you are not required to obtain a certificate of existence, unless you're forming a foreign corporation or LLC.

What's with these mailers I get saying I need new legal documents?

There are scam companies out there that try to convince you to obtain a certificate of existence, labor law posters, or other legal requirements to "complete your setup." If you have your approved articles, EIN, licenses, and governing document, you're set. Furthermore, if these types of notices did not come from the North Carolina government from within the state of North Carolina, they're scams.

Here are a few things you almost never need to purchase:
- Labor law posters (they're free from 1-800-NC-LABOR)
- Certificate of existence
- Rubber stamp
- Stock certificates and register
- Registration on any websites or lists

What is Piercing the Corporate Veil?

Corporations and LLCs provide a shield, or a veil, that separates your personal assets, like your home, from your business debts. This is the limited liability aspect of owning a company, and the protection is fairly ironclad.

The protections do not exist when a court permits a creditor or a plaintiff to do what is called "piercing the corporate veil." This piercing happens when a court determines that the liability protection is not maintained either through some type of fraud or by not following the statutory and common law requirements of the liability protection.

Some examples of when this piercing can happen include when the company is merely an 'alter ego,' when corporate formalities are not followed, the company was improperly capitalized, the company was just a façade, or the company (or company owners) committed fraud in its creation or operations.

What business licenses do I need? Where do I get business licenses?

Business licenses are always changing and they vary based on where you live, what industry you're in, and whether you offer certain products or services.

In North Carolina, to determine which licenses you need, you should call the BLNC business counselors. Their number is (800) 228-8443. The counselors provide their service free of charge.

After I form my company, what other legal needs might I have in the beginning?

After you complete your formation, you also need to create your governing document, any standard contracts, and legal policies and documents for employment (if you have employees). Governing documents and employment matters are covered later in this book.

If you have a lease or are purchasing space, you should have that reviewed as well. Any large purchase or lease, any contract that binds you for a longer period of time, and any contract that you don't understand should be reviewed by an attorney.

Do professionals get protection from LLCs or corporations?

Some. Since most professional liability comes from the actual actions of the professional, an LLC or corporation will not protect as much as other areas. On top of that, there are laws that prevent professional service provides from disclaiming the liability that arises from their professional actions.

LLCs and corporations have a liability shield that protects the owners from things they didn't directly do. This includes contracts, employee liability, premises liability (slip and falls), and some governmental liabilities.

What professionals get from LLCs and corporations is more often than not the beneficial tax treatments that come with them over sole proprietorships.

Should I own real estate in a company taxed as an S corporation?

Probably not. There's a huge advantage to owning real estate in a company taxed as a partnership or disregarded entity. That said, there may be reasons you want an S corporation taxation that supersedes other reasons.

Can a sole proprietorship be taxed as an S corporation?

No. The S corporation election can only be made by corporations and LLCs that meet specific criteria.

How can I identify a scam when setting up my business?

Scams are abundant, and when you list your address on a publicly viewable website, you open yourself up for all of them. Although I can't prepare you for all of them, here are a few to look out for:

- Labor posters. They're free. Don't pay for them.
- Certificates of Existence. Unless you're filing in another state as well, you do not need this.
- Working capital or business loans. If they call you, that's a red flag. Especially watch out for robodialers.
- "Experts" without a proven track record. If you have a specific need, you can usually find someone who is great at that particular need. The generalists who over promise and under deliver are there to take your money and provide a modicum of feedback that anyone who has ever been in business can provide.

I want to set up an investment company. What structure should I use?

There is no certainty because different circumstances lead to different resulting taxes and necessary structure. That said, most investment companies are looking at the LLC structure taxed as a disregarded entity or as a partnership. The reason for this is twofold.

The primary reason to choose an LLC with disregarded or partnership tax is that the taxation is pass through. This means that the tax keeps the same treatment as it came in with without additional company level taxation. This means that royalties, capital gains, and dividends keep their beneficial tax treatment to the owners whereas corporations have to either pay out the money as wages or pay the corporate tax rate prior to distributing profits to the owners.

The other reason is the ease of the structure. LLCs have fewer formalities and easy to setup and maintain. In North Carolina, for the most part, these formality differences are negligible.

How much does it cost to have Law Plus Plus form my LLC or corporation?

At the time this book was published, the Law Plus Plus price was $400, which includes the name search, articles of incorporation or organization, EIN, and your starter governing document. You get everything you need to open your bank account and get started.

NONPROFITS

What is the difference between a nonprofit and a for-profit company?

Nonprofit and for-profit companies are more different than they are alike. They are each subject to a distinct set of laws. Because of the nature of what nonprofits are, they're subject to a stricter set of duties.

The major difference between the two types of entities is the concept of ownership. Whereas for-profit companies are owned by their shareholders or members, nonprofits are <u>managed</u> by their boards of directors. There is no "ownership" in the same sense as for-profit companies. Because nonprofits are not owned, there cannot be payments based on any perceived ownership in a nonprofit.

They are both subject to distinct set of tax regulations as well. Nonprofits are not subject to a company level taxation, and since there are no owners, there is no ownership level taxation. Salaries and wages are, of course, taxable for the recipient.

You also may not sell a nonprofit under any circumstances. Even selling a director's seat is illegal in most cases.

What is the difference between a nonprofit and a charity?

A nonprofit is a state-created entity. In North Carolina, we have nonprofit corporations. These nonprofit corporations are subject to a very unique set of statutes that outline the governance and operations of the nonprofits, officers, and directors.

A charity is an organization that has been recognized by the Internal Revenue Service as a public charity. The charity tax election is a specific tax treatment opposed to an entity type.

In North Carolina, not all nonprofits are charities. Both types may receive donations, but only donations to charities may be deducted from the donor's tax liability.

What is a 501(c)(3)?

A 501(c)(3) charity is a tax status recognition by the Internal Revenue Service. A charity is specifically defined under Section 501(c)(3) of the Internal Revenue Code. Organizations may elect 501(c)(3) charity tax status if they're formed and operated "exclusively for religious, charitable, scientific, testing for public safety, literary, or educational purposes, or to foster national or international amateur sports competition, or for the prevention of cruelty to children or animals."

To become a 501(c)(3), the nonprofit must file form 1023 or 1023-EZ with the IRS, meet all the requirements of the form, and pay the filing fee.

What are the classifications of 501(c)(3)?

The exempt purposes in section 501(c)(3) include "charitable, religious, educational, scientific, literary, testing for public safety, fostering national or international amateur sports competition, and preventing cruelty to children or animals."

Charitable, in this case, is the broadest exempt purpose, which includes "relief of the poor, the distressed, or the underprivileged; advancement of religion; advancement of education or science; erecting or maintaining public buildings, monuments, or works; lessening the burdens of government; lessening neighborhood tensions; eliminating prejudice and discrimination; defending human and civil rights secured by law; and combating community deterioration and juvenile delinquency."

What are the other 501(c) classifications?

There are dozens of other 501(c) classifications that range from broad business organizations to specific teachers' retirement fund associations. A full list can be found through the IRS website at www.irs.gov.

What is the advantages of having the 501(c)(3) election?

There are two major advantages for a 501(c)(3) election: donations from the public and grants. A 501(c)(3) election also provides a level of legitimacy and a different type of tax filing. Without one of these reasons, making this election can be very cost prohibitive.

Where do I get more information on 501(c)(3)?

The internet is full of information about filing for charity status; however, if you want pointed advice, you should speak to an attorney who focuses on this area of law.

If you're looking for good sources of information beyond an attorney's help, check out www.irs.gov, www.501c3.org, www.ncnonprofits.org, and www.lawplusplus.com.

What is form 1023?

Form 1023 is the application for recognition of exemption under section 501(c)(3) of the Internal Revenue Code. You use this same application for private foundations and public charities alike. You complete this form and all required supplements in order to gain the recognition.

What is form 1023-EZ?

Form 1023-EZ (now exclusively an online application) is used for nonprofits seeking public charity status that do not and will not exceed $50,000 in contributions in their first few years. The application is much simpler and quicker than the full form 1023.

What information do I need to have before filing for 501(c)(3) status?

Form 1023 has some specific requirements, so you should prepare these prior to beginning the application.

First, you need to have a fully formed nonprofit company or association in order to file for recognition by the IRS. This process includes your articles of incorporation, employer identification number, and the drafting and ratification of your nonprofit's bylaws.

Beyond the formation requirements, you will also need a conflict of interest policy, a budget for the first three years (or revenue and expenses for the current year and past 3 years), resumes for your directors, and a narrative of your charity's activities and fundraising activities.

How many board members do I need for my nonprofit?

Under North Carolina law, you are only required to have one director. Best practice for having your 501(c)(3) recognition granted is to have at least 3 nonrelated directors.

Can I sell my nonprofit or 501(c)(3)?

No.

Can I have a for-profit/nonprofit partnership?

Yes, but there needs to be clear protections in place to preserve the independence and integrity of the 501(c)(3) nonprofit. These protections should include as much transparency as possible.

Can I have a nonprofit own LLCs or corporations?

Under IRS rulings, yes, a 501(c)(3) nonprofit charity can own LLCs. Under North Carolina state law, there is also no restrictions on this practice. However, having a for-profit structure like LLC under a nonprofit corporation can lead to an added layer of complexity and some unintended consequences.

Most nonprofits either create subparts of their own organization or create affiliated nonprofit organizations when they want subsidiary-style structures.

What is an executive director?

The executive director is the most common term for the chief officer of the nonprofit. In the for-profit world, this position would be referred to as a president or CEO.

The executive director is responsible for the day-to-day operations and management of the company. Whereas the board of directors gives broad direction, the executive director is the manager for all day-to-day operations.

Can the executive director be on the board of directors?

Yes, but there must be a clear delineation between duties as a director and duties as an executive director. The nonprofit also needs a conflict of interest policy in place to ensure that the executive director does not abuse his or her position on the board of directors, especially when it comes to the decisions of employment or compensation for the executive director.

What yearly requirements does my nonprofit have?

There are two major yearly requirements for nonprofits: taxes and meetings. A nonprofit must file their tax forms, or tax postcard every year. This is done with IRS Form 990 or 990-EZ depending on the revenue of the nonprofit.

The nonprofit must also conduct an annual meeting each year. This annual meeting should be used to appoint board members and the executive director. Although they're only required once per year, you can have as many board meetings as your bylaws allow.

What do I need to do to solicit donations?

If you're soliciting on your own nonprofit's behalf, you need to file for a charitable solicitation license. Fortunately, your first year costs nothing.

If you're soliciting donations on behalf of someone else, you'll need to file the charitable solicitation license as well as report annually to the Secretary of State.

How do I obtain a solicitation license?

To obtain a charitable solicitation license, you need to go to https://www.sosnc.gov/csl/Licensing.aspx, log in, and submit the initial application. The entire application can now be submitted online for both the initial filing and renewals.

How much does it cost to have Law Plus Plus set up my nonprofit?

At the time this book was published, Law Plus Plus's flat rate price of $300 covers the name search, articles of incorporation, EIN, and starter bylaws for a nonprofit. This does not include the application for recognition of 501(c)(3) status.

How much does it cost to have Law Plus Plus file for my 501(c)(3) status?

This depends on two things: (1) how much in gross receipts will your nonprofit have and (2) how many hours of volunteering are you willing to do to pay for a portion of your cost?

At the time this book was published, the base rate at Law Plus Plus for filing for 501(c)(3) status is $1,800 for nonprofits grossing less than $50,000 for any of their first three years and $3,250 for nonprofits grossing greater than $50,000 for any of their first three years.

Law Plus Plus also has a program where you can pay part of your bill by volunteering at an approved charity. This requires a significant time commitment, but can cover up to half of your legal fees. You should ask an attorney at Law Plus Plus about this program before assuming you will qualify.

GOVERNING DOCUMENTS

What is a governing document?

Governing documents are those legal documents that set the policies and procedures for the company, establish the company's officers and management, and define the rights and responsibilities of the owners.

The main types of governing documents are articles, bylaws, operating agreements, and partnership agreements. The articles of incorporation or organization are a unique variety of governing document that stand out from the others because they are filed with the Secretary of State. Because of their public nature, minimal information is usually included in these.

Should I use bylaws or an operating agreement for my business?

If you have an LLC, you will use an operating agreement. If you have a corporation or nonprofit corporation, you will use bylaws.

Do I need a governing document?

If your company is an LLC or corporation, yes, you are required to have a governing document. However, if you do not have one and are operating as an LLC, you will have default operating agreement provisions under North Carolina law. If you are operating as a corporation or nonprofit, there are no default bylaws provided by statute.

What goes into bylaws?

Bylaws are the governing document for corporations and nonprofit corporations. What goes into the bylaws depends on whether you are a corporation or a nonprofit corporation.

For both types, you will need to include information on how meetings on conducted, the officer positions and their duties, any governance policies, how board deadlock is resolved, and the miscellaneous boilerplate that appears in most contracts like choice of law.

One of the most important provisions included in both types of bylaws is how the bylaws can be changed. It's somewhat up to you, but always keep in mind that nonprofit bylaws can only be changed by the board and that shareholders have many rights when it comes to changes that affect their interests.

Nonprofit bylaws will also need provisions on what happens upon dissolution, how the nonprofit maintains its nonprofit status, and if it isn't elsewhere, a conflict of interest policy.

For-profit bylaws will need information on how investments are made, when dividends are paid (if ever), and information about shareholders' rights and responsibilities. You should include, in your bylaws, your shareholders' right to transfer stock if you don't have other documents specifically for shareholders' rights and responsibilities.

What considerations should I have for my bylaws?

There is no standard form for bylaws (no matter what LegalZoom says). There's no point in drafting bylaws if every one of them were the same. Your bylaws should reflect your particular needs, wants, and situation.

When drafting bylaws, you should be thinking about all the worst-case scenarios as well as your own company culture in every provision. Some very important considerations include how ownership is divided, what to do in case of disputes among owners or management, when owners are permitted to transfer their stock, how the bylaws can be modified, how to add stock for investment or new shareholders, what types of stock exist, when are distributions made to shareholders, what other duties do shareholders owe to the company, and what happens if an owner leaves or the company shuts down.

What goes into an operating agreement?

An operating agreement is, at its core, a contract between members of an LLC on how to run a company. Because of this, there are very specific things that should be included.

The most important parts of the operating agreement include who owns what portion of the company, how ownership can be transferred (if at all), who manages the company, how management is decided, what rights and responsibilities each member has, how disputes are handled, how to handle members that leave or disappear, how profits and losses are allocated to the members, and any operational details you want strictly enforced going forward.

What considerations should I have for my operating agreement?

An important difference between LLCs and corporations is the fact that LLC owners can allocate their profits and losses in any way they want. The profits and losses do not need to be proportional to ownership interest.

Additionally, LLC owners cannot be W-2 employees whereas corporation owners must be W-2 employees. This is the nature of the separation between owners and managers that corporations have that LLCs do not. In North Carolina, if you do not specify otherwise, all owners of an LLC are managers. Be sure to define the managers and their respective duties in your operating agreement if you want to limit any owner's authority.

One of the considerations is whether to measure ownership in percentages or in "units." It makes no difference from a legal standpoint, but functionally, if you plan on adding ownership in the future, this will dictate how that ownership is added and the impact of the new proportions.

Under North Carolina law, there are also certain information rights that all owners have, no matter what you put in your operating agreement. Keep this in mind if you're bringing on an owner you otherwise wouldn't want to give access to the financial information for the company.

What if I don't have an operating agreement or bylaws?

If you do not have an operating agreement in your LLC, you will be forced to use the default rules provided in the North Carolina Limited Liability Act. These are very generic rules, but you are otherwise not subject to any negative consequences.

If you do not have bylaws in a corporation or nonprofit, you will be in violation of the law. What this means is that you may be subject to civil penalties or some personal liability if your company gets sued. Having bylaws in a for-profit corporation is a corporate formality that must be followed in order to maintain your limited liability protection.

A nonprofit without bylaws would not be approved for charitable status under the IRS charitable recognition (501(c)(3)) and will not be in compliance with North Carolina's Nonprofit Corporation Act.

Are there any formalities to ratifying the bylaws or operating agreement?

Yes, but they're minimal. An operating agreement must be signed initially by all members of the LLC. Bylaws must be ratified in a meeting of all shareholders of the corporation and they must be signed by an officer of the corporation. The corporation must also keep minutes of the meeting in which the bylaws were ratified.

For all future updates, changes, or amendments to your operating agreement or bylaws, these same formalities will apply unless you define other ones in your governing document.

Do I need to file my operating agreement or bylaws with the State?

No.

Do my bylaws need to be notarized?

No.

How do I amend my operating agreement or bylaws?

An operating agreement may be amended by unanimous approval of all members by default. If the operating agreement provides for a different mechanism to amend the operating agreement, that provision will apply. For example, you can set amendments to only require 2/3s majority vote and that would be valid in most cases.

A for-profit corporation may amend its bylaws through its board of directors except where the bylaws require shareholder vote or the change effects a portion of the bylaws that was otherwise enacted by the shareholders. Additionally, shareholders may amend, repeal, or update any portion of the bylaws unilaterally without the board of directors. In all these circumstances, the shareholders or board of directors may alter how the bylaws may be amended. If that provision is enacted by the board of directors, the shareholders may change it, but if that provision is enacted by the shareholders, the board of directors may not change it.

In a nonprofit corporation, you need to obtain majority vote of either the board of directors when there are no members in the nonprofit or majority of members at a meeting where 10% of more of the membership is present. You bylaws may set for higher percentage vote or quorum, but not lower.

Who can see my bylaws or operating agreement?

In a for-profit company, only those people you give permission to can see your bylaws or operating agreement. These are not filed anywhere and are typically a private document; however, if you have a court case revolving around your bylaws or operating agreement, they may become public record as part of that case. Owners will always have the authority to see your bylaws or operating agreement. Typically, banks will require a copy to open a bank account as well.

In addition to your board of directors in a nonprofit, any members your nonprofit has will have the authority to see your bylaws. The nonprofit does not have to make its bylaws available to the public, though it will have to submit them to the Secretary of State's office or Attorney General if either of those offices demand to see them.

Certain grants and other places that work with nonprofits may require a copy of your nonprofit bylaws.

What is the difference between bylaws and articles?

Although they can contain some of the same provisions, articles and bylaws are very different documents. The articles have certain requirements and must be filed with the Secretary of State's office. These are open for inspection by anyone and changing them requires filing additional papers with the Secretary of State. For this reason, you generally want to keep your articles broad. The bylaws are easier to change and are generally private. Therefore, you can include a lot more operational information than you would in the articles.

Are there any things I cannot include in my bylaws or operating agreement?

Yes. Plenty.

First things first: in most cases, if you put something in your bylaws or operating agreement that is not legally permitted, it won't cause you criminal harm. Instead, these provisions will simply be unenforceable. Some provisions, however, will open you up to further liability if there is ever a court case revolving around that or similar provisions. Furthermore, any ambiguity in your operating agreement or bylaws tends to increase the amount of time litigation takes.

Here are some things you should not include:

- Anything that limits your owner's ability to access the books and records in an LLC.
- Anything that gives one owner or one group of owners the power to take away value, ownership, or rights from the other owner(s).
- Restrictive   covenants   (non-competes/   non-solicitations/ nondisclosures) that are overly broad or established merely to prevent competition.
- Anything that requires any person commit an illegal act or an act that subjects that person to civil or criminal liability.
- Unlimited transferability of ownership.

- Any provisions that subject non-owners to obligations.
- Any provisions that conflict with your company's articles.
- Provisions that are overly complex or unlikely to be followed.

What governing documents do I need for a sole proprietorship?

None.

What governing documents do I need for a partnership?

In order to form a partnership, you do not need a governing document; however, you should have a partnership agreement to constrain the rights and responsibilities of each partner. Without a partnership agreement, there is no limit to the authority of each partner, and you could see unlimited personal liability for the actions of your partners.

What governing documents do I need for a nonprofit?

In North Carolina, nonprofits are nonprofit corporations unless they are specifically unincorporated nonprofits. Nonprofit corporations need bylaws.

What are the differences between corporation bylaws and nonprofit bylaws?

Aside from just functional differences in how nonprofits and for-profit companies are run, the major difference between nonprofit bylaws and corporation bylaws are the provisions pertaining to shareholders.

The ownership provisions will change because nonprofits do not have ownership. The distributions portion will change because nonprofits do not give out distributions in the same sense that for-profit companies do.

There are also typically provisions regarding transferring ownership in bylaws. Nonprofit bylaws will not have these provisions.

In a nonprofit, your bylaws will likely also contain provisions on how to meet your mission, a dissolution clause that specifies where the assets go, and a conflict of interest policy of some form.

Biggest mistakes you see made in governing documents?

I've seen so many mistakes in operating agreements, bylaws, and partnership agreements. These mistakes are made by attorneys and non-attorneys alike. The biggest mistakes almost always come from trying to be too complicated.

Here are a couple examples:

- One operating agreement required that the members enact a new, more complete, operating agreement within one year of the one I was reading. That was three years prior. The operating agreement also stated that there was no consequence for not enacting a new operating agreement. Furthermore, this one stated that no decision on the company could be made without unanimous approval. There were five members, and it was a nightmare.

- A two person LLC had five officer positions, each with its own form of checks and balances among the other officers. For example, the CEO could make decisions about staffing, but the CFO could veto that decision if he or she decided vetoing was in the best interest of the company. All-in-all, the checks and balances ended up like a complicated game of rock, paper, scissors, and the positions were divided among only two people!

- One company decided to divide payments based on the absolute most complicated formula I've ever seen. I cannot, to this day, tell you what the ultimate intent was there, but the accounting had to have been a nightmare.

Keep in mind that, in order to change a governing document, you need unanimous approval or the level of approval required by that governing document, if one is specified. That means that bad situations can be made worse by owners who have no interest in making the changes necessary to fix a problem.

What is a morality clause?

A morality clause is a provision included in some company operating agreements, bylaws, or equity agreements that that puts restrictions or expectations on owners outside of business restrictions or expectations. Failure to follow the morality clause can result in a forced buyout or kicking an owner out of the company.

Morality clauses vary wildly depending on what the owners value. A lot of them aren't even enforceable, but the can deter certain behavior and provide incentives to follow the rules.

These clauses can include any number of things, but some of the most common include: (1) limitation on illegal activity, (2) limitation on being accused of honesty crimes like embezzlement, (3) punishment for performing acts that reflect poorly on the company, (4) adultery, (5) or even limitations on use of social media. Depending on the punishments, standing of the owners, or way in which the process is administered, any of these could be enforceable or not.

What is the cost to have Law++ draft my operating agreement?

At the time of this publication, a standard operating agreement would cost $800. Law++'s standard operating agreement covers the requirements of most North Carolina LLCs. So far, only about 5% of LLCs formed by Law++ have required anything more advanced than our standard operating agreement.

What is the cost to have Law++ do my bylaws?

At the time of this publication, standard for-profit bylaws can be drafted for $800. These bylaws include most standard provisions that a vast majority of corporations need. If your corporation needs something more advanced, it would cost extra.

EMPLOYMENT

What requirements are there for my first hire?

You're required to do a few things prior to bringing the employee on board. These vary by industry and location to some extent.

Federal Withholdings.

In order to comply with federal withholdings requirements, you need to set up an electronic withholding account.

State Withholdings.

Similar to the federal withholding program, you also need to set up a state withholding account.

Unemployment Insurance.

For your very first fulltime employee, you're required to carry unemployment insurance for the protection of that employee and all future employees. You can usually get your unemployment insurance through your regular business insurance agency or through a program associated with a payroll company.

Worker's Compensation Insurance.

Some companies are required to have worker's compensation insurance for its first hire whereas the majority of companies must carry this insurance at three or more employees.

Register with State New Hire Program.

Pretty simple. Register your employee with the state's New Hire Program.

Post Required Notices.

There are labor law notices you need to post. Fortunately, they're free and the Department of Labor is happy to guide you through this. Call 1-800-NC-LABOR for more details.

Tax forms: I-9, W-4, NC-4

Every employee, before starting work, must complete these forms. They prove immigration/citizenship status, and declare the employee's federal and state exemptions from withholdings from income tax.

Tip: A payroll company can guide you through most of these. An HR company or employment attorney can guide you through all of them. 1-800-NC-LABOR is also free and can provide a lot of guidance.

Recommended Other Things:
- Set up Orientation Program
- Set up Quarterly/Monthly Reviews
- Create Employee Handbook
- Create Standard Employee Offer Letter
- Create Standard Employee Contract
- Create Process by which Employees can be Fired

What is worker's compensation insurance

Worker's compensation insurance is a type of legally required insurance that covers your employee's hospital bills, time off of work, and other costs and expenses in the unfortunate event of a work injury. This does not provide the employer with any coverage as a result of the injury, only the employee.

Worker's compensation insurance is required for all companies once they have three or more employees, and it is required for the first employee in certain industries (usually the higher risk industries). Regardless of if it is legally required, it is recommended to carry this insurance for your first hire.

What is unemployment insurance?

Unemployment insurance is a legally required insurance for any company that has at least one employee. This protects the employee's income in case of a layoff or downsizing. It does not cover employees in for-cause terminations.

Unemployment must be applied for by the employee after termination, and the employer has the opportunity to contest any claims by former employees.

Employees qualify for unemployment coverage only after working for an extended period of time, and they can only qualify to receive unemployment benefits if the employee is looking for work and while he or she is not otherwise receiving an equivalent salary.

Unemployment is a complicated area of law that should be handled by someone familiar with this field should you need to defend against a claim.

What are withholdings?

Withholdings are when an employer takes a portion of money out of its employees' paychecks to prepay income and FICA taxes on employees' behalves. Employers are legally required to do this for their employees, whether that employee is full-time, part-time, seasonal, or temporary. Salaried and hourly employees alike must have taxes withheld from their paychecks. Failure to properly withhold can result in very large fines and penalties.

What is the difference between an independent contractor and an employee?

The simplest way to explain the difference between independent contractors and employees is that employees are a part of the employer's business whereas independent contractors own and manage their own businesses. That contractor's business can range from a sole proprietorship to a corporation with thousands of employees.

There are complicated analyses to determine which way a worker must be classified for the IRS and Department of Labor, but the most important factors are generally who controls how work gets done and whether the work is a core part of the employer's business.

Employers do not withhold taxes from independent contractors' payments, nor do the employers provide worker's compensation insurance or employee benefits. The downside is that if you misclassify, you will own back payments for taxes, worker's compensation insurance, unemployment insurance, benefits, and large penalties.

For more information on the difference, check out this Law Plus Plus blog: http://lawplusplus.com/2013/12/31/employee-or-independent-contractor-irs-version/.

Can I have unpaid interns?

Yes, but there are strict rules for having unpaid interns. Not paying employees who rightfully should get paid can result in owing back wages and very large fines and penalties.

In order to be an unpaid intern, the worker must be in a purely educational role. Also, that intern cannot supplant what would be a paid position. Mundane tasks such as making an intern get coffee will likely push him or her into the realm of a misclassified worker.

A quick test for unpaid interns is whether they are more work than benefit. This test isn't close to perfect, but this is a safer route.

Every time you have an unpaid intern, you run the risk of that worker filing a claim for back wages. To avoid this, make sure your internship program is clearly education in nature from the outset.

What is a non-compete?

A non-compete is a type of restrictive covenant found in different types of contracts. In the employment context, a non-compete is meant to prevent unfair competition from salespersons, managers, or employees who know technical or business information that could unfairly harm the employer if used against them.

A non-compete will many times look like this: "Employee shall not during the term of employment and for a period of two years after employment, engage in the business of dentistry within a 25 mile radius of the employer." Because of the way North Carolina interprets non-competes, well drafted ones tend to look a lot more complex than this example.

What a non-compete is not is a mechanism to prevent any competition from former employees. Therefore, non-competes are rarely applicable to unskilled, non-sales, positions like cashier unless that employee had access to proprietary business or technical data.

What are the criteria for a valid non-compete?

There are a plethora of considerations when drafting a valid non-compete; however, the basic criteria require that it is reasonable as to geographic territory, time, and scope of the limitation. A non-compete entered into as part of an employment agreement must be accompanied by new consideration, whether that is a new job, promotion, bonus, cash, or new perks of employment. Finally, these non-competes must be narrowly tailored to protect a legitimate business interest.

A non-compete in a sale of business, franchise, or partnership context can be more broadly drafted. All non-competes in North Carolina must be valid on its face. No court will redraft or reinterpret you non-compete if it is otherwise invalid.

What is a non-solicitation?

A non-solicitation is a type of restrictive covenant found in contracts, many times in employment contracts, to prevent an employee from reaching out directly to customers, vendors, or employees in order to get those customers, vendors, or employees to leave the employer and join the former employee.

These many times will look something like this: "Employee agrees that during employment and for a period of two years after employment, Employee shall not solicit, directly or indirectly, any employees, customers, or vendors of employer."

Non-solicitation agreements are usually used in conjunction with a non-compete.

The purpose of a non-solicitation clause is the protect the employer from losing customers, vendors, or other employees to a former employee upon their departure.

What are the criteria for a valid non-solicitation?

Non-solicitation clauses are interpreted in much the same way the non-compete clauses are analyzed, except that they do not need to be reasonable as to territory and scope because their territory and scope is absolutely reasonable (being exactly where the customers are). These agreements must still be reasonable as to time and designed to protect a legitimate business interest. A legitimate business interest is usually easy to prove because the courts have held that customer connections are a legitimate business interest worth protecting.

Because they're treated as non-competes in most circumstances, they must also be made with new consideration, which means as part of a new job, a raise, a bonus, new benefits, or new job perks.

There are very few cases out there contesting a non-solicitation, and they are usually upheld as reasonable, as long as they're not non-compete clauses in disguise.

Similar to a non-compete, these non-solicitation clauses only apply to employees who could unfairly compete with the employer through the actions limited.

When is a nondisclosure (NDA) appropriate?

Nondisclosure agreements are restrictive covenants made as part of a contract to prevent the unauthorized disclosure of a trade secret or proprietary information. These trade secrets can be confidential information, business plans, pricing information, customer lists, or other types of intellectual property that the disclosing party does not want the public to obtain.

NDAs are appropriate when you have a piece of previously undisclosed information or other type of intellectual property that you want to be able to share in a limited capacity with a third party or employee. You can use them to prevent the third party from disclosing this information to others or using it for their own use or benefit.

In an employment context, you can use an NDA to help prevent employees from stealing your customers or copying your trade secrets, business plans, or other important information.

NDAs are not appropriate if the information you're trying to protect has either already been shared with this person or is publicly known. The NDA will not be protective in those cases. NDAs will also not protect from the disclosure of easily discoverable information, regardless of if the public knows.

What is at will employment?

In North Carolina, at will employment is the default. This means that the employee can be fired for any non-discriminatory reason. The alternative is a term agreement. In that case, an employee is guaranteed employment for a period of time with predefined conditions.

What is the right procedure for firing an employee

There is no one right way to fire an employee; however, there are things you should do to help protect yourself from wrongful termination claims or claims for unemployment.

First, you want to have quarterly or monthly reviews where you address any performance problems and create a plan for improvement. That way, if the plan isn't met, your employee has been warned and you have a documented history of the issue.

Second, you want to document everything. Be sure to include the reason why the employee is being fired. If the termination is for cause, you can let the employee know why, but you are under no obligation to do so. Letting your employee know why he or she is being terminated may help or hinder a case against you for wrongful termination or a claim for unemployment. When in doubt, work with your employment attorney or HR professional to craft the right message.

Third, do not debate the termination. Your word is final. You do not have to explain yourself or give your employee an opportunity to be heard on the subject. This back-and-forth typically leads to legal complications. Remember that everything you say can be used against you in court.

Finally, have a witness with you. When you fire someone, they're typically not happy. You will want a witness to protect you in case that employee fabricates a story of something that did not happen, namely discrimination or harassment.

In all situations where you have to fire someone, you want to be the most calm person in the room. You want to ensure that you stick to whatever script you decided on ahead of time and do not give that employee any reason to doubt your decision.

Use your best judgment when it comes to whether or not to take any extreme measures like having security escort the person from the building or mailing their belongings to them. You only want to use these measures when you think the employee poses a threat to other employees or your business.

Some circumstances warrant on-the-spot termination such as theft, physical violence, sexual harassment, gross insubordination, or things clearly forbidden in the employee handbook.

How do I protect myself from unemployment claims?

You can never be absolutely protected from unemployment claims when you let an employee go, but there are many things you can do to mitigate the risk. Documentation is your best friend when you have employees. You want to document any performance issues and the plan you provided the employee to correct those performance issues. This will help you demonstrate a pattern and the employee's failure to meet the requirements set for him or her. These performance issues should be discussed quarterly or monthly with every employee you have during reviews. You should also have separate meetings any time there is a new or unresolved issue with any employee.

When you terminate someone, you want to document the exact performance issues they were being terminated for because a person cannot claim unemployment if they are terminated for cause. They can, however, argue that your stated reason wasn't the real reason they were terminated. Therefore you want to have as much evidence as you can ready to fight that claim including a documented history of performance issues and witnesses, if possible. A clean, and organized, personnel file will make this process super easy.

One of the most creative strategies to helping prevent an unemployment claim that I've seen is helping that employee find a new job. A lot of companies find it cheaper to pay career coaches to help find new jobs for former employees than to pay unemployment claims. These are, of course, employees who were let go, not terminated for cause.

You can also use severance agreements to pay your employee a certain amount of money over a period of time in exchange for waiving any unemployment or wrongful termination claim. These are perfectly valid so long as they're not made under duress or fraudulently agreed to. A good way to avoid fraud or duress is to give the terminated employee a week or two to review the agreement and get back to you.

When can an employee file for unemployment?

A former employee can file for unemployment when he or she was an employee of a company for a certain period of time and was terminated without cause. In other words, unemployment applies to employees who are laid off who met certain duration and/or salary requirements. Each state has different requirements. If you need to file for unemployment, you should contact an attorney who focuses on this field.

Many former employees file for unemployment even if they don't believe they qualify. Their hope is that they'll win the department of labor case, get a settlement, or the former employer won't contest it. Sometimes these results happen.

Do I need labor posters?

If you have employees, yes. They can be obtained for free from the North Carolina Department of Labor by calling 1-800-NC-LABOR.

What are some best practices for having employees?

Because there are so many things you need to consider when having employees, and the laws and best practices are always changing, you should have an attorney or human resources professional on retainer to help you navigate this area of running a business.

Some of the best practices to always follow include:

- Maintain immaculate records.
- Address problems immediately.
- Conduct performance reviews at least quarterly.
- Don't treat your employees like you're one of them. Be the boss.
- Let your employees bring ideas and issues to you or someone who can address them in your company.
- Ensure that every employee knows what to expect in disciplinary practices, termination, corporate culture, and other policies and procedures. Be consistent.
- Maintain your personnel files as though they'll be read in court some day.

Can I record my employees?

You can only record your employees in conversations with you. North Carolina is a one person consent state. That means that as long as one party in a conversation consents to being recorded, that conversation may be recorded.

You cannot secretly record your employees when you're not in the conversation; however, you can let them know prior to employment that they will be recorded at all times. Think of those call centers where every phone call is recorded.

Secretly recording your employees often times leads to a hostile work environment, so be careful with this strategy.

Can my employees record me?

Yes. North Carolina allows the secret recording of another person as long as one person in that conversation consents to the recording. Whoever is recording is going to consent.

Your employee cannot, however, record you where that employee is not in the conversation.

Furthermore, for trade secrets, you can limit the ability for your employees to record conversations.

Is my former employee entitled to his or her personnel file?

In North Carolina, not really. There are certain things they're entitled to see, but those are very limited in scope. If, however, the employee files a lawsuit and requests their file in discovery, the court will likely require that you hand over anything that isn't some form of trade secret.

The lesson there: Even though your personnel files are confidential, they may still appear in court. Don't write anything in them you wouldn't want a judge to see.

What can I or can't I say about former employees?

This is a complicated question that different employment lawyers will give vastly different answers to. There are a few things you absolutely can say:

- Date hired and when the employee left or was fired.
- Whether or not you would rehire this person.
- Ending salary.
- Duties and responsibilities when employed.

Here are the things that are to be avoided at all costs:

- Anything untruthful.
- Telling someone the employee was fired for committing a

crime if that employee was not convicted of that crime.

- Disclosing any medical or mental health issues about the employee.

And, finally, here are the grey areas. For these, it is situational or depends on your own preference.

- Reason for termination. You should have a succinct reason that is objective and provable. For example, if your employee was terminated for not showing up to work three days in a row, you can prove that. If your employee was terminated for wasting time in the bathroom, that is significantly harder to prove (and document).

- Job performance. It is important for this one that the job performance you speak about is documented, objective, and provable. If not, it can come back to hurt you if you harm the employee's ability to gain future employment. For that reason, most employers avoid this topic.

All in all, you're not required to say anything about a former employee. The most defensive strategy I learned from my 11th grade trigonometry teacher. When my parents asked how I was doing, Mr. Labeots responded, "Richard has the highest test grade in the class."

My parents pressed on. "How's his homework grade?" They'd ask.

"Richard has the highest test grade in class," Mr. Labeots repeated.

The lesson learned here is pick a script and stick with it.

"Tom was employed here from January 5, 2017 through February 26, 2017."

"How did he do?"

"Tom was employed here from January 5, 2017 through February 26, 2017."

They'll get the picture and you won't be liable.

MERGERS & ACQUISITIONS

How do I buy or sell a company?

At its simplest, buying or selling a company is just like buying or selling any asset. In this transaction, one party gives money in exchange for the other's company. There is, however, a lot you should do to protect yourself whether you're buying or selling.

Generally, acquisitions begin with a nondisclosure agreement and a request to view the books and records of the company. After an initial inspection, the buyer can make a conditional offer to purchase. That offer is often made with a significant number of conditions. Each of these conditions can spoil the deal altogether or adjust the purchase price one way or the other.

The conditional offer goes by many names. It is called a memorandum of understanding, letter of intent, asset purchase agreement, or company purchase agreement. The asset purchase agreement or company purchase agreements are the more formal versions and typically contain all of the conditions for the deal. They're typically the most expensive and most negotiated portion of the entire deal.

After this offer is accepted, it becomes the agreement. The parties then enter into due diligence. This is the formal fact-finding portion of a sale, and the purpose is to satisfy or verify those conditions from before. Often, a purchaser is required to provide a down payment or "earnest monies" in order to begin the due diligence process. The agreement will specify when and why that down payment can be refunded, but there are very limited reasons why it can. The down payment not only protects the seller from having his or her time wasted, but also compensates the seller for not entertaining any other buyers.

After due diligence is completed by both parties, they conduct a closing where the bill of sale, promissory note, asset transfer agreements, and any other documents necessary are signed and payments are made in the manner specified in the asset purchase or company purchase agreement.

In most of these transactions, there are still ways in which a buyer or seller can back out of a deal even after closing if certain warranties, representations, or covenants are not met.

At any point in the acquisition, the buyer and seller are able to renegotiate the original deal; however, they can only renegotiate if both agree to do so.

What is an asset purchase versus a company purchase?

Asset purchase agreements and company purchase agreements aim to do the same thing: transfer a business from one owner or set of owners to another in exchange for some value. Functionally, however, these two types of agreements result in very different processes.

A company purchase agreement has the simpler process. In this type of agreement, the seller transfers the shares or ownership interest in the company to the buyer for the purchase price. This is easiest because the company remains in existence and only one type of asset is transferred: the ownership. Ownership in a company is personal property, the easiest type of property to transfer.

An asset purchase agreement involves a more complicated process. In this transaction, all or substantially all of the assets of one company are transferred to another company in a single transaction or series of transactions. This transfer leaves the selling company as an empty shell and the new company with all the seller's assets. The resulting company has a new tax id number and is protected from almost all of the liabilities of the selling company.

See the diagram on the next page to get an idea of how the money and assets flow between the companies in an asset purchase.

Company 1	Company 2	Transaction
Assets	(Doesn't Exist)	Starting Point
Assets	$$$$	Form new Company 2 and fund it with enough money to buy Company 1
$$$$	Assets	Exchange money for assets in an asset sale
Empty	Assets	Distribute money to Company 1 owners
(Doesn't Exist)	Assets	Dissolve Company 1

An example of an asset sale would be if the seller were a retail store and it sold all its inventory, customer lists, pricing data, business plans, employment agreements, lease terms, etc to the buying company. You can likely see why this is more complicated than just selling the shares of the retail company.

In an asset purchase transaction, the buyer will need to reestablish nearly every contract. This includes a new lease, sign new employment agreements, sign new vendor agreements, establish new payroll accounts, obtain new insurance, and setup new customer contracts.

In a company purchase, there are fewer contracts that need to be revisited. The entity still exists; therefore, unless there's a clause that invalidates the contract after a sale like this, the contract stays valid and enforceable. It's called a "change of control," which means new owners of the company. Mortgages commonly include this provision.

The buyer can never be completely free of liability. Although asset purchase agreements greatly limit liability for the purchaser, liabilities such as sales tax, payroll tax, mortgages, liens, and UCC-1 financing statements can follow the assets into the new company. Consequently, the buyer should focus on these things during due diligence.

Additionally, a court may have the authority to reverse the transaction or hold the parties liable for certain liabilities. The court may do this in cases of fraud or errors in the transaction. This is usually called fraudulent transfers.

Tax treatments for these transactions are also different. In a company purchase, all taxes stick with the company. In an asset purchase, only certain taxes follow the assets, like sales tax and sometimes payroll tax. Corporate taxes will not follow the assets. Additionally, in an asset purchase, the parties must file form 8594 to determine what classifications the assets are in. This matters for depreciation and future sales because certain asset classes have different capital gains and depreciation treatments.

What type of sale is best for a buyer?

Though every situation is different, buyers generally prefer an asset purchase agreement because it greatly limits their potential liability.

What type of sale is best for a seller?

Though every situation is different, sellers generally prefer a company purchase agreement because it is simpler and quicker. This saves the seller money. It also eliminates the need for the seller to dissolve the selling company after the sale, which can be another potentially painstaking process.

What can I do now to help with my future sale?

Most sellers struggle getting all the documentation together in a clear and concise manner. To help with this, you should maintain all your records in one place, keeping them as organized as possible. For financial reporting, you need an accountant who prepares regular reports. He or she should also go through your books to ensure they're easy to review. Generally acceptable accounting principles (GAAP) is important to follow if you ever plan on selling.

If you know there is a sale in the immediate future, you can gather the most important documents now. These include your annual tax filings; profit & loss statements; payroll records; currently open contracts; all policies and procedures; legal documents; and any past, current, or threatened litigation. These items are almost always requested in due diligence.

How can I maximize my company's value?

Maximizing your company's value is a very complicated process; however, there are some things that are sure to increase your value no matter what you company is.

First, you can ensure that your expenses are low. Keep your

company as lean as possible to show maximum profit.

Second, keep good records. Sloppy records make buyers uneasy whereas organized records tend to alleviate concerns.

Third, maximize how much reoccurring revenue you have. Reoccurring or ongoing revenue is more predictable and therefore worth more to a potential buyer. Risk lowers the price.

Fourth, set up documented systems. If the company is ready to run without you in it, your systems alone will be worth a large amount of money to a potential buyer.

What reasons might an acquisition fail?

Buying or selling a company is a very complicated transaction. It is also a very risky deal for the buyer. Therefore, there are a lot of reasons this transaction could fall through.

The most common reason this type of transaction falls through is because expectations are not met. This usually results when the seller over promises and under delivers. If you promise a multi-million dollar company, it better be making at least two million in revenue. Be sure that every promise you make can be backed up with documentation as the buyer will want that.

Acquisitions fail when the buyer realizes there's more risk than the buyer is willing to take on. This is sometimes the fault of the seller, sometimes the buyer's, and other times no one's fault at all. Occasionally, the buyer simply had low expectations for risk and became educated during the process.

It is actually common that acquisition fail because they cannot legally be completed. There are sometimes contracts like mortgages or leases that make it impossible to complete the sale. If these obligations cannot be transferred, it may be impossible for the buyer to take on the business. Because of this, the seller should approach these parties ahead of time to ensure the obligations can be transferred.

Some sales fall through because the buyer and seller cannot come to an agreement on one or more material terms. For example, buyers look for indemnification for all past liabilities and a seller may not want this long term liability hanging over his or her head. It is impossible to predict what terms of the sale are material to each party, so it is very hard to prepare for these situations. The best you can do is list all of your material terms up front. Addressing material terms too late can be disastrous.

Remember that acquisitions of private companies are not adversarial. Both parties should be happy at the conclusion of the deal, except in the cases of some minority owners.

What are representations and warranties?

Representations and warranties are the most important promises in the sale of a business. They are promises that, if violated, can result in the non-violating party reversing the transaction. For example, if the seller warrants that there are no pending lawsuits against the company and there happens to be an undisclosed lawsuit, the buyer can reverse the transaction and get the down payment and all other monies back. Representations and warranties are very carefully worded to protect each party.

What is due diligence?

Due diligence is the process of investigating the company to be bought or the buyer's ability to pay and/or run the company. This is generally done after the asset purchase or company purchase agreement is signed. This process is used to verify certain conditions and provide a level of ease to both parties.

Typically, a buyer is looking at all past tax records (including sales tax), payroll reports, profits and loss reports, employment records, all litigation, all larger contracts, leases, mortgages, liens, threatened legal action, inventory, and anything that stands out or is important to the buyer. The seller typically only looks to whether or not the buyer can pay as promised.

During due diligence, the price is sometimes adjusted to reflect new findings. Sometimes, new agreements are entered into to protect one or both parties regarding new information that is discovered.

It is very common to update the indemnity provision throughout the process.

What should I look for when conducting due diligence?

Some of the most important things to look for when conducting due diligence are the following:

- Income tax records
- Sales tax records
- Litigation and threatened litigation (including on the job injuries)
- All employment records including performance reviews, terminations, unemployment statuses, and any employment contracts
- All long term or larger contracts to ensure they can be transferred and that they're not about to expire
- All liens, mortgages, UCC-1 financing statements, or loans
- Profits and loss statements
- Inventory records
- Customer lists
- Any negative press or reviews
- Outstanding gift certificates or other liabilities
- Anything that is important to the buyer

How long should the due diligence period be?

Due diligence periods are directly correlated to the complexity of the transaction. Larger companies have larger amounts of information to go through, so those generally take longer.

In very few circumstances should your due diligence period be less than three months because that's about how long it takes to get a certificate of good standing from the department of revenue.

Moving too quickly can result in a nightmare later. Be sure to cover all your bases before committing to the transaction. Sometimes, the excitement convinces potential buyers or sellers to overlook some otherwise damning information.

Due diligence may last several "rounds." It is common for the buyer to discover something that leads to further questions. He or she may then request more documentation from the seller to satisfy those questions. This can go on until the buyer is satisfied or the seller refuses to continue supplying more information.

What documents are associated with a company purchase?

Every transaction is different, but most will see at least the following:

- Nondisclosure agreement (NDA)
- Letter of intent or memorandum of understanding
- Company purchase agreement
- Bill of sale
- Equity transfer agreement
- Promissory note

There can be plenty of others depending on what comes up in due diligence and what is important to both parties.

What documents are associated with an asset purchase?

Every transaction is different, but most will see at least the following:

- Nondisclosure agreement (NDA)
- Letter of intent or memorandum of understanding
- Asset purchase agreement
- Bill of sale
- Asset transfer agreement
- Intellectual property transfer agreement
- Promissory note
- Form 8594 Asset Acquisition Statement

How do I shut down my business?

Shutting down a business is fairly straightforward. First, you have to approve the dissolution by the owners (however your governing document requires approval). This includes the plan for distributing the assets and who is in charge of that process. Second, you file your articles of dissolution with the Secretary of State. Third, you notify known creditors directly of the dissolution. Fourth, you notify all unknown creditors through publication in a major newspaper in the county (or counties) your business is in. Fifth, you distribute the assets to the creditors and then to owners if there are any assets left. To provide for unknown creditors, you can hold money in the company until the end of the notification period.

If you distribute money to the owners and then find out there were creditors that were owed, your owners may be personally liable (up to the amount they were paid) for those debts.

Is a nonrefundable down payment common when buying a company?

Yes and no. The down payment should still be refundable under specified conditions like fraud, violation of representations or warranties, or the seller cancelling the transaction. Absent these circumstances, a "nonrefundable" down payment is fairly common. You are welcome to contract other conditions upon which the deposit will be refunded. Consider misrepresented inventory, poor performance prior to the closing, or leaked details of the sales if they apply in your situation.

Your deposit not only pays part of the purchase price, but it also prevents the seller from entertaining other buyers. A seller cannot take multiple down payments simultaneously, and the agreement should specify how long you are the sole person eligible to purchase.

What is the role of a broker when buying a company?

Business brokers are only responsible for pairing a potential buyer with a potential seller of a business. They should not provide any legal advice, yet they can provide help figuring out what each party wants or help with pricing.

Brokers should absolutely not be preparing legal documents or reviewing due diligence for the buyer or seller unless the broker is also an attorney or CPA (for some documents).

How much does a typical acquisition cost in legal fees?

The simplest purchase would cost at a minimum of $2,000. You should expect a greater cost for any level of complication or due diligence. There's no way to quantify the cost without knowing the exact circumstances of the sale.

A couple of key elements that go into complexity include the following:

- Company sale versus asset sale
- Seller's years in business
- Number of revenue streams
- Number of employees
- Number of owners
- Different types of assets
- Physical locations
- Regulated industries
- Larger transactions
- Messy books and/or records
- History of lawsuits or insurance claims
- Real property
- Vehicles
- All schedules of insurances, licenses, and permits

Should the seller stay on as an employee after selling the company?

This depends on your situation, but you can include this in your agreement. You can also have the seller stay on as an independent contractor consultant. Different rules apply to each of these situations.

If you need to be trained on running the company, it is highly recommended that you include some sort of provision in the agreements that require the seller to stay and train you.

Ideally, the seller would have provided documentation that explains most elements of the company. This limits how much need there is for ongoing input from the seller.

Should the sale of a business include a non-compete?

Yes.

Besides a non-compete, how can a buyer protect him or herself when buying a company?

It is important to not only include a non-compete, but also non-solicitation, nondisclosure, and non-disparagement protections when buying a company. Each of these restrictive covenants protects something separate and should be use specifically for their appropriate uses.

It is possible (and recommended) that you include a series of ownership transition events. These are a good way to transfer the trust the customers had for the seller to the buyer. In these events, your customers will have a chance to ask questions of both the buyer and seller at the same time.

Beyond those things, the buyer should also ensure that there are appropriate representations, warranties, and indemnity provisions included in the agreements. That way, if the seller were lying or there were unforeseen issues with the transaction, the buyer can back out of the deal or be appropriately compensated for any losses.

To mitigate risk, the buyer can also pay over time and keep a portion of the sale held in escrow. Holding the money in escrow is essentially insurance. After a specified period of time, the escrow money can be released to the seller. These strategies help remove the potential that the seller spends all the money leaving the buyer with no recourse for fraud or failed covenants or warranties.

What is a hostile takeover?

A "hostile takeover" is a pretty popular term in movies and TV. All it really means is that one or more parties acquire enough ownership in a company to overthrown the leadership without the prior leadership's consent. In corporations, this usually involves buying up large amounts of stock on the stock market or from private shareholders who want out. It can also involve creative uses of stock options and proxies to have enough voting interest to appoint a new board of directors.

In an LLC, it will all depend on what the operating agreement allows. Similarly in partnerships, it depends on what the partnership agreement allows.

INTELLECTUAL PROPERTY

What is intellectual property?

Intellectual property is a group of property rights. They specifically revolve around the right to control the usage of certain creative, intangible, or inventive things. The types of intellectual property include copyrights, trademarks, patents, trade secrets, and goodwill (sometimes).

What is a copyright?

A copyright is the right to control who and how a creative work can be used. A copyright is automatically granted when someone makes something unique and creative in nature. This ranges from pieces of art to dance moves. In order to have a copyright, however, the work must be in a tangible medium. Ideas are not copyrightable.

There is also a registered copyright that comes with extra protections and a presumption that you were the first to create this particular work.

If we're talking about creative works and preventing people from copying them, we're talking about copyrights.

What is a trademark?

A trademark is the right to prevent other persons or companies from using the same or substantially similar symbol or slogan in the same industry and geographic region. This right is conveyed to prevent the dilution of a company's goodwill with the public.

A registered trademark (with the USPTO) comes with a significant amount of statutory protections as well as United States wide territory. An unfiled trademark (common law trademark) comes with only regional territory and less protections than the registered one;

however, the common law trademark is free.

In order to obtain trademark protection, you must establish the regular use of the mark to represent your business, product, or service. To establish this, you must consistently use the mark for a decent period of time. In trademarks, you do have to use the mark before you can protect it.

You can also file an "intent to use" trademark. What this means is that you will be establishing the consistent use of the mark for your business, product, or service, but you haven't yet. This essentially gives you an extra year of protection prior to your actual usage.

States also have their own registered trademark processes that come with state-wide protections. You wouldn't need to file for a state registered trademark if you already have a USPTO trademark.

Some trademark designs can also gain copyright protection because the design is creative in nature, but that protection is distinct from the trademark protection.

What is a service mark?

A service mark is the same as a trademark, except for a service instead of a product. It can be registered in the same way as a trademark.

What is a patent?

A patent is a type of intellectual property that gives you total control over who can use an invention. This is the strongest of the intellectual property protections, but it is also the hardest to obtain.

Patents actually have their own separate bar exam, so only patent attorneys can give advice on the obtaining and use of patents. Law++ does not handle patents; however, we do have relationships with patent attorneys.

What is a trade secret?

A trade secret is a term given to proprietary or confidential information belonging to a company. Trade secrets do not have any registered protections. It comes with statutory protections so long as you take appropriate steps to protect the trade secrets such as the use of NDAs and properly storing the information. Trade secrets are protected by federal and state laws.

Keep in mind that trade secrets do not include things that could be subject to any whistleblower act or things that have already become public record.

What is goodwill?

Goodwill is the term for the intangible value placed on the reputation of a company. Because goodwill is an asset to the company, companies do a lot to ensure its value is kept strong.

When should I file for a trademark?

You should consider filing for a registered trademark when you've been using a particular mark to represent your business for at least 3 months. You must also plan on protecting this mark should anyone infringe upon it. With trademarks, if you don't protect them, you lose them. Therefore, if you want trademark protection, you must ensure it is worth putting the time and money into keeping it.

The trademark process, if done with an attorney, will cost a minimum of $1,000.

When should I file for a copyright?

Right away. If you plan on using a piece of work to generate money, you should register it with the copyright office. It's a very cheap process compared to the advantages you get.

When should I use an NDA?

When you want to protect trade secrets or a patentable idea before it is patented, you should use an NDA. In order to obtain either of these protections, you have to ensure they are not already publicly known. Once you'd told people without these protections, you begin running the risk of not having any protection at all.

Additionally, it is a good idea to use NDAs to protect confidential information about your business that may not amount to a trade secret. Think of things that would really hurt your business if your customers or competitors knew. These should be protected.

Are there any laws that protect me and my trade secrets?

Yes, the North Carolina Trade Secrets Act and the similar federal statutes were enacted to protect trade secrets from unlawful or malicious disclosure. Other states have similar protections as well.

What does public domain mean?

Public domain is a specific copyright term that means that work is no longer subject to anyone's copyright protection. Something can become public domain either by the copyright holder explicitly releasing it to the public, the copyright expiring, or the copyright holder not enforcing his or her copyright over an extended period of time.

If something is on the internet, is it public domain?

No.

If a copyright owner makes something public domain, can he or she reverse that decision later?

It depends, but not in most circumstances. If the copyright owner made the work public domain, but included stipulations that allowed for him or her to reverse that decision, then it is possible that it can be brought back out of public domain. This sounds as difficult as putting the toothpaste back in its tube.

Generally, once something is public domain, it remains that way forever.

What does creative commons mean?

Creative commons is a specific type of licensing for copyrighted works. This can mean a variety of things, but broadly speaking, it means that the copyright holder has allowed certain usage of the copyrighted work for free as long as specific criteria are met.

If I give attribution, can I use a piece of copyrighted work?

Not necessarily. Giving attribution alone does not necessarily give you the right to use someone's copyrighted work.

What is fair use?

Fair use is an exception to the copyright rules. What this means is that under certain circumstances, you're allowed to use a portion of someone's copyrighted work for free. There is no bright line rule for what qualifies as fair use, but some of the criteria used to examine this include whether the usage is commercial in nature, the amount of the original work used, whether attribution is given, and the context around the usage.

If I mail myself my work of art, does that count as evidence for proving my copyright?

This is sometimes referred to as a "poor man's copyright" and although it can count as evidence, it is very poor evidence. You're better off uploading your work to a server you have no control over, publishing on Amazon, or using a plethora of witnesses. Obviously, registering with the US Copyright Office is the best approach, and it isn't that much more expensive than mailing to yourself.

What is "work made for hire"?

Work made for hire is a specific designation that means that the employer or purchaser of the intellectual property owns the copyright for any developed copyrightable works. This happens by default in an employer-employee relationship.

For independent contractors, work made for hire is a bit more complicated. In order for the arrangement to qualify for work made for hire status, this designation must be explicitly stated in writing and the work being made must fit within a few select categories. Some of these categories are open to interpretation, so it would be impossible to clearly outline them in this book.

A good alternative to the work made for hire designation in independent contractor situations is by having the independent contractor assign the copyright or provide a license to use the work.

LITIGATION AND CONFLICTS

Are trials like you see on TV?

No. They're really boring by comparison.

What does the litigation process look like?

The litigation process is usually very linear. It starts with the filing of a complaint and is followed shortly by discovery. Between filing the complaint and the trial, there are also usually a few motions filed. In North Carolina you will also have to attend court order mediation or arbitration.

After the complaints are filed, motions are heard, and all the discovery requests are complete, you finally get to the trial portion. At trial, each side calls witnesses and makes their case. At the trial's conclusion, the judge or jury renders its decision.

If either party is displeased with the result at trial, he or she may appeal the decision to the appellate court.

What is small claims court?

Small claims court is a special court with relaxed rules of evidence for cases demanding less than $10,000 (in most NC counties). Certain types of cases cannot be heard in small claims court, no matter how much the case is for.

Either party may appeal the small claims ruling by appealing to the district court. This appeal completely eliminates the decision made by the small claims court and starts the process over anew.

Small claims cases are vastly quicker than those cases in district or superior court.

What's the difference between state and federal court?

The primary difference between state and federal court is the type of cases they have jurisdiction over. Federal court has jurisdiction over things granted to it like maritime law, patent violations, and issues regarding the US Constitution. Additionally, federal court can have jurisdiction over cases between parties of different states where the amount in controversy is **greater than** $75,000.

Each court has its own rules of evidence and rules of procedure. On top of that, there are state rules and then local rules for each particular court and each judge may set his or her own rules as well.

What's the difference between district and superior court?

The primary difference between district and superior court in North Carolina is the amount in controversy. Superior court handles all cases where the amount in controversy is greater than $25,000. There are also types of cases and hearings that are only handled by one court or the other, but in the business law realm, it almost always comes down to amount in controversy.

Do I need an attorney to represent me in court?

If you're a business, yes. If you're an individual, it is recommended. Under North Carolina law, businesses are required to have an attorney represent them in court. Individuals are not required to have an attorney, but the court will not be lenient on individuals who fail to follow the rules of evidence or rules of civil procedure.

What is arbitration?

Arbitration is easiest described as a miniature trial with relaxed rules of evidence that is presided over by an expert in the industry instead of a judge. The arbiter is usually a former judge or attorney who practiced in the area that is being argued. After hearing both sides, the arbiter makes a decision which can be entered into the court as a final decision. The arbiter's decision may be final or it may be appealable, depending on the contract or reason the parties are in arbitration.

What is mediation?

Mediation is a formal negotiation process lead by a unbiased mediator. The mediator is usually an attorney who is specially trained to conduct mediations. During mediation, both parties sit in separate rooms and the mediator goes back-and-forth until a settlement can be reached or the parties reach an impasse.

If a settlement is reached, the parties sign an informal settlement agreement and arrange how the formal settlement agreement is to be drafted. The important thing is that all material terms are addressed during the mediation.

Typically, during mediation, both parties pay their own attorney, and they share the cost of the mediator.

What is a settlement?

A settlement is a private agreement that dictates that both parties drop their cases against each other in exchange for some value and/or terms. Whereas the results of a case are typically public record for anyone to view, a settlement can be completely private. In some circumstances, a judge may need to approve a settlement, but usually not in business cases.

What can be included in a settlement?

Anything that isn't illegal can be included in a settlement agreement. Basically, you should include every important concern in the settlement agreement. A couple of very common terms to be included are:

- No admission of fault.
- Confidentiality of the terms of the settlement.
- Release of any and all claims against the defendant.
- Consent Judgment – An agreed upon judgment if one party fails to uphold his or her portion of the settlement.
- Payment now or over a period of time.

Do courts have to approve settlements?

No, not in private business cases. In certain other areas of law, yes.

What happens if I lose my case?

If you lose your case, you can choose to accept the result allowing the other party to collect on that judgment, or you can appeal the case to the appellate court. If you choose to accept the result, the prevailing party can use the sheriff to attach liens to and foreclose on your property.

What is the difference between trial and appellate courts?

Whereas the trial court listens to all the facts and the witnesses, the appellate court almost exclusively deals with the law without hearing new facts. The trial court is called the finder of fact. That power is given to a jury or a judge depending on the case.

In the appellate case, the judge or judges will be tasked with finding out if the trial court made a mistake, either evidentiary, abuse of discretion, or misapplication of the law. Appellate courts may also determine that the law is wrong.

The structure and rules are also different. In North Carolina, most appellate cases are not even heard orally by a judge; they're handled exclusively through the written record and briefs. The rules are also far more strict.

Finally, the parties to the trial rarely even have to attend an appellate court case because the appellate court has no need to get their input.

Do I need to attend every hearing?

No. Only some hearings require the parties to attend. Most hearings are argued between the attorneys and they convey the results to their clients. If you represent yourself, then you must attend every hearing that you care about winning.

What are the rules of evidence?

The rules of evidence are a set of rules to ensure that only credible evidence is presented to the court. These are fairly strict in their application, so it is important to know and follow them in court.

Repeatedly failing to follow these rules can result in fines (or sanctions) from the court. Also, each party is required to object when the opposing party attempts to enter evidence into the record that is in violation of the rules. Absent that objection, the court may allow the evidence.

What is a complaint?

The complaint is the formal document that starts the case. It must lay out who the parties are, how the court has jurisdiction, the alleged facts of the case, the causes of action, the demanded relief, and the signatures of those presenting the case.

A verified complaint is one where the complainant swears under oath to the accuracy of every fact and demand in the complaint.

Complaints must contain enough alleged facts to fulfill the elements of whatever cause of action the complainant is raising or that complainant will lose his or her case prior to trial.

What is an answer?

The answer is the response to a complaint. In the answer, the responding party must either admit or deny each line. The respondent may also state that they do not have enough information to either admit or deny each line.

The responding party may include a counterclaim with his or her answer. Filing the answer accepts jurisdiction; therefore, if the responding party believes the court lacks jurisdiction, he or she must raise that objection prior to answering. Failing to answer in the statutory timeframe will result in a default judgment.

What is a counterclaim?

A counterclaim is where the defendant sues the plaintiff under the same or similar set of facts. In a breach of contract case, you almost always see a counterclaim for breach of contract.

Some counterclaims are "compulsory" which means the defendant must make the claim or forever lose his or her ability to seek redress for that harm. Counterclaims are typically compulsory when they arise out of the same or similar set of facts.

What is discovery?

Discovery is the formal process by which you can gather facts from the other party, under oath, before going to trial. The party that receives the discovery requests has only a limited time to go through and answer each item or provided the requested information or documentation.

Discovery can primarily be broken down into four types: (1) requests for admission, (2) interrogatories, (3) requests for production, and (4) depositions. There are others, but they don't come up in business law.

Requests for admission are when you are asking for an admit or deny response. Interrogatories call for longer responses in the opposing party's own words. Requests for production are when you're asking the opposing party to turn over physical evidence such as records, photographs, and more. Depositions are verbal interrogatories, and they can be used against people other than just the opposing party. Depositions are transcribed afterwards, so they become a written record. Requests for admission, interrogatories, and requests for production are all usable only against the opposing party. If you want information or documentation from people not involved in the case, you can ask, subpoena, or depose that person.

What is a motion?

A motion is the formal way to ask a court to do anything for you. Anytime you need the court to adjust anything or make a ruling, it must be made in the form of a motion.

What types of motions are there?

There are dozens of types of motions. Some of the more common ones in business cases are summary judgment, sanctions, default judgment, entry of default, dismiss, set aside judgment, new trial, and demurrer. As mentioned, there are dozens, and some do not have common names like these.

Why is the other party allowed to drag out a case?

This is a question I get often and it is hard to answer. There are many reasons a case can be delayed, and a court is fairly inclined to grant these delays. Every party will be granted at least one extension to a deadline and usually one continuance for the trial as well. If there's a good reason, the court will typically grant additional extensions and continuances.

The best answer I can give is because the court is lenient when it comes to granting more time for either party.

What if I think the other party is lying?

If the other party is lying under oath (either in discovery or on the witness stand), you can try to catch them in the lie through more evidence or more questions. If they are lying in negotiations, there's nothing you can do.

If under oath, you have two options: (1) press charges for perjury or (2) use the lie to impeach the person. To impeach someone means to negate their credibility as a witness in front of the court. This helps your case when the other party is impeached. Most instances of lies are not met with criminal charges for perjury, but it is an option.

What can I do to be better prepared for court?

To be best prepare for court, you should ensure that your documentation is detailed and accurate. This should include any accounting records you keep. Ensure your attorney knows every detail of your case, even if you think it may not be relevant. A good way to lose a case is to have your attorney blindsided during trial.

If you're going to be a witness, it is important to remember you should only answer the question that is asked. If it is your attorney asking, he or she will have you elaborate. If it is the other attorney asking, he or she will likely keep trying to pull more information out of you that could hurt you. You should continue to answer honestly, but only the question asked.

It is also important to know that "I don't know" or "I don't remember" are perfectly valid answers if you don't know or can't remember. It is better to state one of these than to make an assumption or make something up. Getting caught in a lie will ruin your credibility and leave you vulnerable to criminal charges for perjury.

What is a deposition?

A deposition is a form of discovery where an attorney is permitted to ask questions of the opposing party or a witness in the case while that person is under oath. The deposition is recorded and then transcribed. It can then be used at trial to impeach a witness or prove a case.

What happens after I win a case?

After you win a case, you get a judgment. The opposing party then has a short period of time to appeal the court's decision. If that party does not appeal, you enter into the collection phase of litigation. Unfortunately, winning doesn't automatically grant payment. You then have to find the opposing party's assets for the sheriff to seize.

Many times, the prevailing party will still settle the case afterwards to speed up the process of getting paid on the judgment. You can also hire collection agencies or private collectors to handle this portion for you for a percentage of the judgment.

How much does court cost?

Court is not cheap. At its cheapest, you're looking at a couple thousand dollars to go through a simple case. More realistically, you're looking at a minimum of $10,000 for a standard business case. The more complicated the case, the more expensive the price tag. There's also a direct correlation between the amount in controversy and the amount you'll pay.

What are some common disputes I should look out for?

Common disputes depend largely on your industry and particular situation. Obviously, if you're a doctor or lawyer, you see more malpractice suits. If you're dealing with a lot of employees, you may see more employment related disputes.

Most every company has to worry about breach of contract cases. These arise when one side of the contract is dissatisfied with the performance or lack of performance by the other side. Frequently, this type of case arises when one side did not get paid.

If you have a partner, or partners, in your business, a partnership dispute is unfortunately very common and generally fairly avoidable. These partnership disputes are also the most costly disputes a company can face.

Someone I'm in a dispute with asked for my insurance policy information. Should I give it to them?

It depends. When someone asks for your insurance policy information, it is likely because he or she wants to make a claim against your insurance. If you're looking to have your insurance cover this claim anyway, it may not make a difference. Otherwise, you may be unnecessarily increasing your insurance premiums if and when that person makes a claim against your insurance.

What is a default judgment?

A default judgment is a type of judgment that results from one side not answering a complaint. Essentially, it is an automatic win for the complainant. Default judgments are slightly easier to set aside than other types of judgments, but generally, you will have to show good reason to set it aside.

ABOUT THE AUTHOR

Richard Bobholz is an award-winning attorney, speaker, business owner, teacher, and dedicated community member. He is the author of several other books, focusing his more recent publications on business and law. Beyond helping his community through these resources, Richard dedicates a significant amount of his time to providing community service and pro bono legal services to the less fortunate in his community.

Richard enjoys running, backpacking, computer programming, writing, eating, and spending time with family and friends.

Richard obtained his Bachelor's Degree in Economics at Michigan Technological University and his Juris Doctorate from the Kline School of Law at Drexel University in 2012.

Richard currently practices at Law Plus Plus, a revolutionary and award-winning law firm that is dedicated to making the legal system easier, enacting positive change in the community, and constantly improving how they operate and the effect they have on their clients' lives and in their profession. With this mission and his genuine approach to the practice of law, he is able to help small businesses, nonprofits, and social entrepreneurs protect themselves and develop their businesses in a deliberate and systematic manner.

Above the degrees and accolades, Richard values his ability to see things from multiple perspectives. This view of the world helps him break down problems into their simplest components and build a solution from that analysis. It is this style of thinking that allows him to be an incredibly valuable resource for his clients.

In 2015, Law Plus Plus was recognized by the American Bar Association for their contribution to pro bono services, taking second place nationwide for their commitment, and in 2016, Law Plus Plus became the first law firm in North Carolina to become B

Corporation Certified.

Beyond those accomplishments, the attorneys at Law Plus Plus also contribute hundreds of hours every year toward community service through programs like Habitat for Humanity, Clean Jordan Lake, the Food Bank, Activate Good and many more.

Richard also sits on the Board of Directors for Activate Good, an amazing organization that promotes and pairs volunteers with causes, creating a multiplier effect in the community. The organization not only supports these nonprofits, but also inspires the next generation of leaders through their Activate Schools program and gives the resources needed to get businesses involved in coordinated days of service for their employees.

INDEX

FREE CONSULTATION

Anyone who brings in a copy of this book is entitled to one free consultation from Law++. This free consultation is subject to availability by Law++, the passing of a conflicts check, and the determination that the firm can help in the particular legal matter.

To redeem your free consultation, please go to www.lawplusplus.com/contact to schedule a meeting with an attorney. Be sure to include that you're redeeming the free consultation from this book in your message.

Hope to see you soon!